JONATHAN DICKINSON'S JOURNAL

Jonathan Dickinson's Journal

OR,

God's Protecting Providence.

Being the Narrative of a Journey

from

PORT ROYAL IN JAMAICA

to

PHILADELPHIA

between

August 23, 1696 *and* April 1, 1697.

Edited by EVANGELINE WALKER ANDREWS
and CHARLES MCLEAN ANDREWS
with a Foreword and New Introduction by
LEONARD W. LABAREE

Florida Classics Library
Port Salerno, Fla. 33492

Library of Congress catalog card number: 61-11399

ISBN 0-912451-00-9

Contents

Professor and Mrs. Charles McLean Andrews, 1940—*Photo by Charles Vergos*

The Jonathan Dickinson Journal when it first appeared in 1699 was valued highly by the Quakers of that time. The instance of Divine intervention as the shipwrecked party faced cruel death on Hobe Sound beach at the hands of the savage Jobes Indians was of such importance that they had the book reprinted fifteen times, often in little leather bound volumes tooled in gold to be treasured and handed down from generations by their families and friends. There were later reprints in Dutch and German.

In 1934, Dr. Charles McLean Andrews with his wife, Evangeline Walker Andrews, leased the old DuBois home on the ancient shell mound south of Jupiter Inlet. Dr. Andrews was a distinguished writer and historian, a professor emeritus of Yale University. He was visited by a former student, Louis Capron, who presented him with one of the rare copies of the Dickinson Journal. He learned that the pre-historic shell mound upon which he lived was the site of the village of Hobe where the Dickinson party was held captive.

Dr. Andrews interest in the Journal led to seven years of intensive research. He died in 1943 but Mrs. Andrews continued the work on the Journal which was published in 1945 with extensive notes. This copy of the Journal rekindled the interest in this inspirational account which is also the first description of the aboriginal Indians of this area. The nearby state park was also named for the courageous Quaker.

Bessie Wilson DuBois

(Taken from the 6th Edition of 1803 and considerably abbreviated from the 1st Edition of 1699 and others.)

Ingratitude towards men, after signal favors received, is, among all civilized people, looked upon with a just detestation; insomuch that the moral Gentiles, in ages past, thought they could give no worser character of a person, than to call him ungrateful: How much more than are Christians (especially in a time of such light as now shineth) engaged to shun this sin of Ingratitude toward their God, whom they sensibly know to be the fountain of all their mercies? And Surely, next to the infinite mercy shown them for Christ's sake, in causing the day-spring from on high to visit their souls, remarkable outward deliverances ought, in a more than commonly remarkable manner, to be the objects of their gratitude to their great deliverer. I must confess, thanksgiving (which is what we poor mortals can return, for the manifold favors we daily receive from him) hath its rise in the heart; and as out of the abundance of the heart the mouth speaketh, how can those who are truly thankful in heart, but render the calves of their lips, in telling their friends and acquaintance, how great things God hath done for them! Nay, they are so affected with such eminent appearances of the protecting hand of Providence for their help, preservation and deliverance, that they are not willing to confine it to them only, but to publish it to the world, that the fame of their GOD may be spread from sea to sea, and from one end of the earth to the other.

But I foresee some persons may be ready to say, here is an account of very strange passages, but of what credit is the relator? May we depend upon his authority, without danger of being imposed upon? To such I answer, he is a man well known in this town (Philadelphia) of good credit and repute, on whose fidelity and veracity, those who have any knowledge of him, will readily rely, without suspecting fallacy. But, that in the mouth of two or three witnesses, every thing may be established, besides him and his wife, a person whose residence, when at home, is in this town, Joseph Kirle, the master of the barkentine in which they suffered shipwreck, a man of honest character amongst his neighbors, had the perusal of it before it went to the press, and approved it. With which I shall conclude, wishing my reader much satisfaction in the reading of it, but never the unhappiness of experiencing, in proper person, the truth of it.

(The author of the Preface is unknown.)

Foreword

THIS narrative of a shipwreck on the Florida coast in 1696 and the suffering and heroism of the survivors was first published in Philadelphia three years later. So great and so sustained was the interest the account aroused on both sides of the Atlantic that it was reprinted no less than sixteen times in England and America, and three times each in Dutch and German translations, all between 1700 and 1869. None of these versions provided any considerable editorial treatment. It remained for the late Professor Charles M. Andrews of Yale and his wife Evangeline Walker Andrews to undertake the first thorough research into the history of the event, the lives of the characters involved, and the subsequent printings of the narrative. They were especially attracted to the subject because they spent many winters after his retirement at Jupiter Inlet near the scene of the shipwreck. Professor Andrews died in 1943, before their edition was quite ready for publication, and it became my privilege, as one of his former students, to assist Mrs. Andrews in the final stages of editorial preparation and in seeing the book through the press in 1945. It was dedicated to their children, Ethel Andrews Harlan and John Williams Andrews.

The long-continued search for new information had been both far reaching and highly successful; the volume which resulted from it contains almost exactly twice as many pages of introduction and appendices as the text of Dickinson's own narrative occupies. A good deal of the material they included has great interest for the historical specialist or the bibliographer but is not essential to the general reader's understanding or enjoyment of the journal itself. The present edition is based directly on that of 1945, but the Introduction, completely rewritten, presents in somewhat condensed form only those topics from the Andrews volume that seem likely to be of interest to that wide reading public of our own time which the narrative most certainly deserves. Of the Andrews appendices the only ones retained essentially unchanged are those which reprint the preface to the original edition of 1699, a contemporary letter, and a note describing the Florida Indians in the seventeenth century.

It has been a pleasure thus to renew my contact with Jonathan Dickinson and the brave men and women who shared with him one of the most extraordinary experiences of the American past. And it is my hope that those who read this little book will gain inspiration, as I have done once more, from the courage and determination they displayed in a time of great adversity.

L.W.L.

Yale University
March 1961

When Valentine Martin, publisher of this newest reprint of Jonathan Dickinson's Journal, asked me to write about the Florida sea islands locale where this epic adventure of the spirit took place, he stirred a deep chord in my own experience.

Again I remembered the Vanished People, whose kitchen middens of oyster shells and rude tools of conch shells and bones I had found scattered along the coasts of Jupiter Island and Hutchinson Island when I had been swamp-roaming in the Twenties and Thirties. And how a dog-eared old copy of the Journal, printed at London around 1772, had brought those people into being again in my mind.

I would push my skiff far up the twisting mangrove creeks that led in from Peck's Lake to the sea beach at the center of Jupiter Island. Although there was an exclusive residential resort developing to the south, today's Town of Jupiter Island, this part and northward to St. Lucie Inlet was sheer wilderness and will remain so, now fortunately under ownership of Florida State Park Service and the Department of the Interior's Fish and Wildlife Service. How amazing it was to come out from the dark tunnels of the mangrove creeks bordered by the twisted trees on their spidery roots into the bright white light of the sea beach, stretching out of sight in both directions — utterly devoid of people.

There were eagles and ospreys, occasional flocks of majestic wood ibises, herons, gulls and man-o-war birds, the tracks and droppings of raccoons and wildcats — but no people. There was the eternal rustle of shells being chewed by the surf, sand fleas digging down frantically in the receding surges, fairy terns dipping for rain minnows, fish striking, sharks finning by, and marks in the sand where giant loggerheads had crawled ashore in the night to lay their eggs on the lip of the dune and back to sea again.

Back from the beach, deep in the cabbage palm hammocks and the mangrove swamps, where still stood some black mangroves 500 years old, it was a place of stillness. Even the surf rustle and the wind went unheard. Even so small a creature as a land hermit crab seemed to make crashing sounds as it dragged its shell across the dry palm fronds of the hammock floor. Once, sitting and musing in the heart of the swamp in a place of dappled sunlight and shadow, I was seized with a feeling of dread. The hair rose on the back of my neck. Something, I knew not what, was threatening. A bear? A panther? Or that most savage of all predators, another human being? I looked all around for a minute, seeing nothing, my fears mounting — until an old dead tree sighed and thundered down on to the forest floor.

There were no people, but one sensed their presence around the shell mounds and deep in the hammocks. I picked up broken shards of their pottery — and wondered. How had they dressed? What sort of houses had they lived in? Had they been afraid? Had anyone been afraid of them?

These Carib tribes that once had their towns and villages on both coasts of Florida — the great kingdoms of the Caloosas and the Tomokas, and the little sub-provinces of the Tegestas, Talakas, Jobeses, Jeagas, Ais along the Indian River and the Timucans to the north — have utterly disappeared. Were they wiped out by disease or war?

No one knows. But we are all indebted to a Friend, Jonathan Dickinson, a Quaker of Jamaica wrecked among them on September 23, 1696, with a company of Quakers, seamen and slaves, for a vivid description of how they looked and how they lived. He was the first to describe in detail these savages who peopled Jupiter Island when the Reformation came ashore. He called them Furies.

And I am indebted to an old gentleman, Captain Charles H. Coe, retired from the Government Printing Office at Washington, D.C., for first introducing me to his ancient copy of Dickinson's Journal or God's Protecting Providence in 1937. The book repeopled my beloved wild islands with the childlike, greedy, sometimes kind, more often cruel, semi-brave but inwardly fearful, simple but withal trying to be cunning Vanished People of this part of the New World.

Most particularly, I am grateful to him for sharing with me this story of that courageous band of shipwrecked people who had fallen among the savages, regarded as fair prey because the Indians thought they were English, not Spaniards — but weren't quite sure. Dickinson has related their trials, indignities and sufferings, made bearable only by their faith in God.

Coe, in his late seventies when I first met him, with a Van Dyke beard and wearing a faded nautical cap, brought his Journal to The Stuart News office where I was working as a reporter. It was a Fifth Edition, printed in antique English type by Mary Hinde at London around 1772, and copiously annotated. He explained that he was retracing Dickinson's route and making a map to show sites of the Indian villages where the shipwrecked people had stayed. Would I help? Indeed I would.

We went down to Peck's Lake in his old-fashioned cabin launch, Buccaneer I, its gunwales lined with grinning skulls — some trepanned by medicine men to let the evil spirits out — which he had taken from various digs on islands up the Indian River. He showed me necklaces of human finger bones, teardrop-shaped Venetian glass trade beads, stone pendants, shell tools and broken pottery which he had exhumed.

"Treasure hunters keep digging into the graves," he complained, "but there isn't any treasure in them."

The Spaniards seized any treasure they got from wrecks. And most of the artifacts are smashed up. They broke a man's possessions when they put them in the grave so that the spirits of his tools could join his spirit."

We were at a mound about midway down Jupiter Island, near where the shipwreck occurred. "No use digging here," he said, surveying the piles of ancient oyster shells. "This is just a kitchen midden, a sort of garbage pile of shells and bones. They buried their dead back in the hammocks, about an arrow's flight distance from where they held their feasts and most often to the northwest. Here, take the shovel and follow me," he said. The old gentleman was uncanny. We went about a hundred yards or so back into the hammock where there was a slight elevation with full-grown palm trees atop it.

"This is probably it," he said in the quavering voice of the aged, pointing to the little hill covered with palms. "They buried their people in sitting position alongside and on top of one another and piled baskets of sand over them. Dig right there," he indicated.

I dug. After only three or four spadesful of sand had been removed, a perfect white skull with finely formed strong teeth and gaping eyesockets seemed to look up into the present from ages past.

"A beauty!" exclaimed Captain Coe. "Your first, I assume. What do you plan to do with it?"

"It's really mine?"

"Of course, you found it."

"Then I'm going to leave it right here," I said as I spaded the sand back and patted it down. "And we'll leave all the rest of them, too. You don't need any more on the Buccaneer. You have plenty aboard to last you the rest of your life."

He was disappointed, but took it like a man. From then on, when I took him to various mounds on the islands, he was content just to find the places and mark them on his map.

Charles H. Coe was a remarkable man. He had been the original editor of the Florida Star, which later became the Titusville Star. He had exposed by pamphlet an "old Spanish fort" at New Smyrna as the more prosaic ruins of a sugar mill. His major literary production was "Red Patriots," a strong defense of the Seminoles, first published in 1898, and credited with eventually righting some of the injustices done to them. A reprint edited by historian Charlton W. Tebeau of Miami was published in 1974 by the Florida Bicentennial Commission.

In the several years that I had the pleasure of his company, visiting numerous old Indian towns on a succession of houseboat launches — he navigated the rivers until he was 89 — I found him a delightful raconteur. His stories made me forget those grinning skulls as we sipped wine and ate oysters on deck. An incurable romanticist, when he was past 80 he developed a one-sided love affair with a young woman he had met at a fishing camp on Lake Okeechobee and wrote lyrical poems to her which he insisted on reading aloud after suppers.

He was a great friend of John and Bessie Du Bois at Jupiter Inlet, on whose place was located the big mound, site of the town of the head cacique (Indian chief or sub-king for this region) where the Dickinson party was first taken to the southward, and whence they struggled north, partly afoot, partly by boats, to reach St. Augustine and eventually Charles Town and Philadelphia.

I finally managed to get Captain Coe to loan me his early Journal. My sister Isabel copied it by typewriter and I practically memorized it. Since then, by good fortune, I have come into possession of two antique editions, the 1803 Sixth which prominently features

Dickinson on the title page, and one of 1826, titled "The Shipwreck and Dreadful Sufferings of Robert Barrow, With Divers Other Persons; amongst the Inhuman Cannibals of Florida," and in small type, "faithfully related by Jonathan Dickenson who was concerned therein." The early books spell it Dickenson instead of Dickinson, printers being as prone to error then as now.

The Journal should qualify as the first American classic. First published in the print shop of Reinier Jansen at Philadelphia in 1699 some 276 years ago — 77 years before the signing of the Declaration of Independence—it is a forerunner of that ringing phrase: "One nation under God . . ."

It seems eminently fitting that this reprint of the Yale University paperback published in 1961, a revision of the more complete book edited by Evangeline Walker Andrews and Charles McLean Andrews, published by Yale University Press in 1945 with a second printing in 1946, should be republished with Yale's permission by a book firm located at Stuart, Florida — so near where the historic wreck occurred. It is also fitting that it should be reprinted in this time of Bicentennial observance.

No other book in America's heritage has been reprinted so many times over so many years — with 16 reprints in English and others in Dutch and German. It was advertised in 1736 as one of the books "Printed and sold by B. Franklin in Market Street, Philadelphia" but no copy of any printing by Franklin has been found. This appears to be the 17th reprint in English, although the book was so popular that research may turn up others.

Why its popularity? Because it spreads the message of a deep, unswerving personal faith in God. The Society of Friends sponsored a number of the editions in America, England, Holland and Germany to spread the doctrine of faith's power over violence.

Faced with death because they were alien English-men — a party of shipwrecked Dutchmen had been murdered to the man up the coast a few years earlier — these people laid down their muskets and prayed to God that He would turn the arrows and blunt the knives of the savages. While they were terribly abused, robbed and stripped naked at times — even cruelly given the leaves torn from their great Bible to cover themselves, most survived. The accusation "Nicka-leer!" or "Englishman!" rang in their ears constantly, but most denied it, a white lie to save their lives. They claimed to be "a new sort of Spaniard bound for the new Spanish colony of Penn's Woods." All except Robert Barrow, the Quaker preacher from the North of England, filled with the "dayspring from on High," who never lied. They feared for their lives when the Indians would try to question Barrow.

Their epic tale should remind us all of the short gap between the comforts we take for granted and the agonizing privations of being without shelter, clothing, warmth, food, potable water, freedom and kindness — to be in the power of the cruel and ignor-ant. We take the filling of our basic needs for granted. A world facing the unknown perils of the nuclear age may be better armed with such faith as succored these brave people.

Back to my sea islands, where the Vanished People are now sitting in eternity in the sand mounds under the palms, I am grateful to Dickinson for letting me see them as they were. His Journal has put flesh on their bones, human flesh, and rapacity and greed and kindness.

Though I may still wonder why they disappeared — perhaps their time had come as it comes time for an old tree to fall in the forest — I now realize that they were feared by those in their power and fearful of those with more power, like Spaniards with muskets. I see them faced with the problem of deciding whether they should kill people of an alien sort, simply because they belonged to a "hostile nation," a responsibility civilized men still must argue with conscience. I see them with their few pitiful belongings of clay pottery, conch shells and bones, which must be broken in the end, their little houses of palm thatch atop the oyster heaps, their food of fish, shellfish and occasional deer, suddenly showered with the riches of a wrecked ship, plain as it was.

They who had food from day to day, if they could find it, plundered the stores and chests of the Reformation. They who had no clothes but bits of deer hide and breech clouts of woven straw with plaited grass like horses' tails behind, snatched the clothes from the shipwrecked.

But they did, on occasion, share their catches of fish and baskets of bitter palm berries. Their women did nurse the Dickinson infant when his mother's milk went dry.

Out in my seashore swamps, when the salt marsh mosquitoes and the sandflies hit in a scalding scourge, I have built smudges of green mangrove leaves and then been forced into the sea to duck under and survive. How did these poor shipwrecked people, stripped naked as jay birds, endure such insect plagues? Back on the edge of the mangroves, the raccoons dig little depressions in the damp sand to get their water. It is brackish and makes you want to throw up — and that is the only drinking water on the sea islands. How did the shipwreck victims stand it?

Fully clothed, with a fire nearby and under blankets, I have shivered under the cruel northwest wind — we call it a "blue norther" — and it was this worst foe of all that took five lives.

Fearful as they were of the armed Spaniards, the

Indians on this coast were not the domesticated sort found around the missions at St. Augustine, amenable to priests. Dickinson notes that two Spanish friars had been burned at the stake on a bluff opposite St. Lucie Inlet some years before. These savages worshipped pagan gods, shaking their rattles, howling hideously and prancing around a painted pole for days far into the nights, as he tells about a ceremony he witnessed at the town of Jece, where he described them as looking "like men frighted, or more like Furies."

He was shocked at their social customs, writing that "these people had no compassion on their own aged declining people when they were past their labor, nor on others of their own which lay under any declining condition: for the younger is served before the elder, and the elder people both men and women are slaves to the younger."

They were a small people, full of jealousy and avarice, threats and bluff, with petty little kings, some overlords of others, seizing what they could and having it seized from them by the stronger, with Spain grabbing the plunder in the end.

And yet they were human beings, all of them, and this is a human story. It's greatness lies in the faith of the Friends and their company, but there are other shining lights that must not be ignored. The Catholic Spaniards sent down soldiers to help the Protestant English reach St. Augustine, outfitted them with food and clothing on credit, and sent them on toward Charles Town with Indian guards through the land of the Yamassees. So human a story. The printer in the first edition put in caps the parting words of the Spanish Governor at St. Augustine, who "wished us well, saying WE SHOULD FORGET HIM WHEN WE GOT AMONGST OUR OWN NATION, and also added THAT IF WE FORGET, GOD WOULD

NOT FORGET HIM."

God was somewhat more personal then than now. He was with the Governor at St. Augustine and He walked with the shipwrecked, differing though their creeds might be.

When I visit my island beaches today, I can see the two savages who rushed up, "running fiercely and foaming at the mouth," to grab two crewmen carrying corn ashore. Dickinson persuaded his company not to go for their guns but to "put their trust in the Lord."

Looking out at my island beach I can see stout Captain Kirle with his broken leg, mending painfully, trudging along supported by his Negro slave, Ben. There's solemn Mister Dickinson and young Mistress Dickinson clutching her infant to her breast, while some Indians run in and out like crows trying to snatch the few rags they have left. Seamen and slaves are strung out in the distance and far, far behind, tottering along, two steps forward, one step back, is the frail wraith of the Quaker preacher, Robert Barrow, walking hand in hand with God. Some Indian boys are throwing shells and flotsam at him. No matter. He has made up his mind that, if it is God's will, he will lay his bones in Philadelphia—and it was; and he did.

A strange procession on an empty beach. They have gone on, but I feel the presence of more people, on the shell mounds, back in the palm hammocks, going up and down the mangrove creeks to spear fish in the river and gather oysters in Peck's Lake. There may even be a dance tonight around a painted pole. The Friends got away from this strange place but the Furies are still there.

By Ernest Lyons
Editor, Stuart (Fla.) News

The Florida Indians Capture the Shipwrecked Company.

Introduction

ONE of the dominant themes running through the early history of this nation concerns men and women who have faced hardship and suffering with dauntless courage. The epic story of settlement and expansion is filled with countless episodes in which those who came before us met danger, starvation, disease, and death bravely and steadfastly in order to win homes on this continent for themselves and their descendants. These incidents—some familiar to all of us, others little known—differ infinitely in setting and detail. Some have happy endings, others are tragic from start to finish; a few involve large numbers of people, most are concerned with small groups of individuals seeking together some common goal. Such incidents were not confined to any single section of the country nor to any one generation of American pioneers; they occurred in all parts of what is now one nation and at all stages of its settlement. They include such experiences as the "Starving Time" in the first years of the Jamestown settlement, the Indian attack on Deerfield on the Massachusetts frontier, the heroic defense of the Alamo, the disaster of the Donner party high in the Rocky Mountains, and scores of other episodes all over our land and throughout the American past.

The swift march of our civilization and the crowding events of recent years have tended to obscure some of these heroic episodes, helping us to forget some of the sufferings and sacrifices men and women underwent in the course of building this nation. The very places where some of these events took place have undergone so much change and development that it is often hard to realize that close to where we are going about our daily affairs may be a spot hallowed by the courage and the sorrows of some other Americans who came here long ago. It is well, however, for us to pause from time to time and consider the price that men and women paid in years gone by for those first footholds on the land we now call ours, and for us to live again, if only vicariously, some of the experiences through which they passed. To do this should give us all a deeper, richer appreciation of our heritage and a renewed courage to face the problems of our own times.

One such episode, less well known generally than it deserves to be, took place toward the close of the seventeenth century along the shores of Florida's east coast. It involved perhaps as mixed a group of persons as any incident of comparable courage and suffering: a number of hardy seafaring men, a few gentle Quakers, and a handful of Negro slaves. There were both men and women in the party, one "aged" man, and two small children, one a baby not yet weaned. They were traveling by water, as they hoped, from Jamaica to Philadelphia when their ship was driven ashore in a heavy storm and wrecked on Jupiter Island, a few miles south of the present town of Stuart. Captured and stripped virtually naked by a band of ferocious and hostile Indians, beaten and almost starved, their lives constantly threatened, the party managed through the help of "God's Protecting Providence," as the Quakers believed, to struggle up the coast some 230 miles to the hospitable Spanish settlement of St. Augustine. Here they were fed and clothed, rested, and then sent on their way by small boat and with a guard of soldiers, but in the dead of winter, to Charleston, South Carolina, and thence by ship to their destination, Philadelphia. The narrative of their adventure, the day-by-day account of their sufferings, of the deaths that occurred among them, and of their final deliverance, was set down by one of the party. It is one of the most vivid and moving journals of heroism and suffering, of patience and courage, to be found anywhere in the long annals of the American past.

The barkentine *Reformation,* Joseph Kirle master, set sail from Port Royal, Jamaica, on August 23, 1696, bound for Philadelphia. On board were a crew of eight mariners besides the master; a Quaker missionary, Robert Barrow; a young Quaker merchant, Jonathan Dickinson; his wife and little baby; a relative named Benjamin Allen; and Dickinson's eleven slaves. Apparently he had chartered the vessel to carry his party and a cargo of merchandise worth about £1500 to the northern city, where he planned to open a branch of his family's commercial business. England and France were at war in 1696 and the convoy system was in effect; hence the *Reformation* was one of a group of a dozen or so vessels sailing together under the protection of the frigate *Hampshire* commanded by Captain Fletcher.

As often happened in those days when ships were completely dependent on wind and weather, the convoy was unable to stay together, and after about a week of drifting calm the *Reformation* lost sight of the other vessels. Forced to pursue its course alone, the barkentine slowly rounded the western tip of Cuba, always fearful of attack by a French fleet known to be in the vicinity, and headed for Havana. As the ship neared that port a sudden squall struck, the boom jibed, and the master was knocked down, breaking his leg. The same afternoon Dickinson's Indian slave girl Venus was taken with convulsions and died a few hours later. At length, on September 19 the wind turned fair and without trying further to reach Havana the *Reformation* headed north for the Bahama Channel, which, aided by the Gulf Stream, carries vessels up past Florida into the open Atlantic.

After two days of good weather the wind backed around and on September 22 a violent storm struck from the northeast. During that night or the next—the account is not quite clear which—the vessel struck and soon ran fast aground close to shore. Waves broke violently over the ship, washing the deck cargo overboard, flooding the cabin, and starting the planking. When daylight came all the passengers and crewmen, including several who were ill, managed to get safely ashore, build a fire, and salvage some of their clothes and provisions from the wreck. The spot where they landed was about five miles north of Jupiter Inlet.

Saved from "the devouring Waves of the Sea," the members of the *Reformation* party were soon menaced by "the more cruelly devouring jawes of the inhumane CANIBALS OF FLOR-

IDA," as the title page of the printed account describes their new predicament. The Indians of that part of the peninsula were a ferocious and brutal tribe—identified as the Jobeses, or dwellers of the Rio Jobe, as the Spaniards called Jupiter Inlet—so primitive in culture that they had not developed even the rudiments of an agricultural economy but depended for their food on fish, oysters, berries, and such other edibles as nature provided. Though they were probably not actually cannibals, Dickinson and his companions thought they were, and this belief added to their terror when the Indians, having discovered the castaways, descended upon them and took them captive.*

These natives had experienced just enough contact with Europeans to stand in considerable awe of the Spaniards, while picking up a few words of their language, and to regard the English (whom they called "Nickaleer") as mortal enemies. Dickinson and the other whites sensed that admission of their true nationality would add to their peril and tried to make their captors believe that they were Spaniards hoping to go north to the settlement at St. Augustine. Solomon Cresson, one of the *Reformation* crew, could speak Spanish and served as best he could as interpreter. But one of the party, possibly Robert Barrow the Quaker missionary, was a little like the young George Washington of later legend: he could not tell a lie, and nearly if not quite gave away the secret. In any case, the Indians stripped their captives almost naked, took away their salvaged possessions, and threatened their lives with menacing gestures. Fortunately the chieftain or cacique (spelled "casseekey" throughout Dickinson's narrative) was a more kindly or moderate man than most of his followers and would not let them inflict bodily injury on the helpless prisoners. But he did insist on their marching southward with him and his people to their wigwam village on the far side of Jupiter Inlet, where the remains of a huge shell-mound still mark the site.

How Dickinson and his companions finally won the cacique's

---

* For a fuller description of the Florida Indians in Dickinson's time, see Charles M. Andrews' account in Appendix C, p. 93.

consent to their traveling northward toward St. Augustine, partly by water in canoes and the ship's longboat and partly by land; how they met up with the survivors of another ship from their original convoy wrecked in the same storm; how they were treated by other Indians along the way; what they suffered from hunger, from storms, from the increasing cold as the fall season advanced, and from sheer exhaustion; how Solomon Cresson managed to get word of their plight to a Spanish patrol far up the coast; how some of the party died on the last desperate stage of the journey just as the safety of St. Augustine seemed almost within reach; how the Spaniards treated the survivors when at length they attained that outpost of European civilization; and how they later made their way in open boats to the haven of Charleston, arriving there the day after Christmas—all this is a story that should be read only in the vivid and moving words of Jonathan Dickinson himself in the pages of this journal. To follow his account is to gain some appreciation of the inner strength that enables men and women to face danger and suffering with courage and determination and, against seemingly hopeless odds, to win through to the attainment of their goals.

Most of those who sailed from Port Royal on the *Reformation* and endured the hardships of the shipwreck and the long journey north remain merely as names on the party's roster that Dickinson entered on the first page of his journal. A few who play conspicuous parts in the narrative, however, were well enough known in their own day to have left other records which permit some account here of who they were and why they had undertaken the voyage. Four men deserve particular notice:

Robert Barrow. Among the members of the shipwrecked party by far the best known at the time was the Quaker missionary Robert Barrow. Born in Lancashire, England, and a mason by trade, he had moved to Kendal, Westmoreland, as a youth. Converted to Quakerism, he dedicated himself to the propagation of The Truth, traveling for twenty-six years through the British Isles and preaching "Jesus Christ the Light of the World." Like many other Quaker missionaries of the seventeenth century, he was severely persecuted, enduring imprisonment no less than seven times, but meeting all misfortunes with patience, meekness, and courage.

Late in 1694 he sailed for America on a missionary journey, leaving behind his wife, the former Margaret Bisbrown, and at least two children. In company with a fellow-evangelist, Robert Wardell, he traveled among the English colonies on the continent and in the West Indies for about a year, reaching Jamaica in April 1696. Both men were affected by the hardships of their travels and by the "scorching heate of the Climate" in the West Indies. Wardell died fifteen days after arriving in Jamaica, and Barrow "had not one dayes health" during the twenty weeks he remained on the island before sailing for Philadelphia with the Dickinson party on the *Reformation*.

Barrow's exact age is not known; probably he was about sixty at the time of the shipwreck. References to him as an "aged man" and as "in ould age" must be understood in terms of the seventeenth century, when life expectancy was so much less than it is today and when any man who had lived half a century was regarded as approaching old age. Certainly Barrow's years of strenuous travel and suffering in the cause of religion must have left their mark. Whatever was the total of his years, his fellow Quakers regarded him as one of their noblest seniors, and his death, April 4, 1697, a few days after he finally reached Philadelphia, was indeed a sad loss to them. In a very real sense they regarded Dickinson's narrative of the shipwrecked party's experiences as an account of Barrow's final sufferings. Though the missionary's name did not appear on the title page of the first edition of *God's Protecting Providence*, as the book was entitled, it was featured equally with Dickinson's in most later reprints, and in time Barrow became in many minds the central hero of the tale. By 1792 one pious publisher, at least, had completely changed the title so that it read in part "The Remarkable Deliverance of Robert Barrow, with Divers Other Persons, from the Devouring Waves of the

Sea, . . . Faithfully related by Jonathan Dickenson, one of the Persons Concerned Therein."

Joseph Kirle. The master of the barkentine *Reformation* made his home in Philadelphia, where he was regarded as "a man of an honest character among his neighbors." Like any typical ship's master of the day he had accepted command of the vessel from its owners and was prepared to sail it at their orders anywhere among the colonies that the commerce of the times required. A few days before the shipwreck he had broken his leg—an accident that Dickinson called, with great restraint, "grievous to him and to us"—and undoubtedly this injury prevented him from assuming a more active role as at least the nominal leader of the castaways. The loss of his ship apparently did no permanent injury to his standing as a competent seaman; after he got back to Philadelphia he received other commands, and Dickinson, as a prosperous merchant in the years that followed, gave him considerable shipping business.

Solomon Cresson. The only member of the *Reformation's* crew, other than the master, to figure prominently in Dickinson's account was the youthful Solomon Cresson. He was of French Huguenot stock, his grandfather Pierre having first fled from Picardy to Sluys in Flanders and then migrated to New Amstel on the Delaware in 1657, two years after the Dutch seizure of that Swedish settlement. The next year Governor Stuyvesant persuaded Pierre Cresson to move to Manhattan, where he became one of the first settlers of the Harlem district. Here Solomon was born in 1674, one of nine children of Pierre's son Jacques. When he was about ten or eleven his father died and his mother Marie soon moved with her children to the Dutch island of Curaçao. Family traditions differ as to how young Solomon spent the next eleven years, but he appears to have undertaken a number of commercial voyages in the West Indies, working with or for an older brother. In any case two things are clear: somehow during his travels he acquired a command of the Spanish language, and somehow he arrived in Jamaica in 1696 in a penniless condition, glad enough to ship as an ordinary seaman on board the *Reforma-*

tion, bound for Philadelphia, to which city the Cressons had by this time moved their home. As the only Spanish-speaking member of the shipwrecked party, young Cresson proved to be of great service to his fellow sufferers.

Settling down in Philadelphia after the Florida experience, Solomon Cresson became a turner and chairmaker with a shop on Chestnut Street. In 1702 he married a Quaker girl, Anna Watson, and became himself a member of the Society of Friends. He died in 1746, aged seventy-two, survived by four of his nine children.

Jonathan Dickinson. The author of this account seems always to have spelled his name Dickinson, though the title page of the first edition and most of the later reprintings rendered it as Dickenson, with that fine disregard of the niceties of spelling that characterized so many printers and writers of the seventeenth and eighteenth centuries.

His family was one of some distinction in England: his grandfather William Dickinson was a clergyman of the Established Church of England, and his uncle Edmund was physician to King Charles II. His father Francis raised a troop of horse in 1654 for Oliver Cromwell's Western Expedition, which seized Jamaica from Spain the next year. Just what important services Francis Dickinson performed in Jamaica during the years of fighting which followed in the island is not known, but it is probable that several grants of land to him during the 1670s and 1680s were, in part at least, rewards for his help in establishing English rule. In Jonathan's lifetime the family estates totaled about ten thousand acres, including two plantations, "Barton" and "Pepper," in Elizabeth Parish, near the Black River, some forty to sixty miles from Kingston and Port Royal. In addition to his activities as a planter Francis Dickinson engaged extensively in commercial business at Port Royal, the island's chief seaport. He was a member of the Jamaica Assembly in 1672, but in the next year, having become a Quaker, he was denied his seat because he would not take the required oath.

Born in Jamaica in 1663, Jonathan Dickinson was one of the

seven children—four sons and three daughters—of Francis Dickinson and his wife Margaret. The son joined in his father's mercantile business at Port Royal and shared with him in the losses that struck all Port Royal merchants when that town was almost completely destroyed by an earthquake and tidal wave in 1692. Yet the family fortunes did not suffer as severely as those of many other Jamaicans did, for when Jonathan embarked, four years later, on the *Reformation*, bound on a commercial venture to Philadelphia, he was able to place on board a cargo worth about £1500, apparently with the intention of using it to open a branch of the family business in the prospering new Pennsylvania community. Meanwhile the young man—he was thirty-three when he sailed—had married Mary Gale of Jamaica; their first child, Jonathan, Junior, was born some five months before the family sailed.

With Jonathan, besides his wife and baby, was his "kinsman" Benjamin Allen (their exact relationship is not known), and eleven slaves. One of the latter was an Indian girl named Venus; another was Cajoe, the small child of the Negro woman Hagar. Including the master Joseph Kirle, the eight other members of his crew, and Robert Barrow, the entire ship's company numbered twenty-five. Of these, the Indian girl died on the voyage and five others succumbed before the survivors of the shipwreck which followed had reached the safety of the Spanish settlement at St. Augustine.

The strength of character and capacity for leadership Jonathan Dickinson displayed during the harrowing weeks on the Florida coast may help to explain the success of his later life. Somewhat uncertain at first whether or not to make his permanent home in Philadelphia, he had decided by 1700 in favor of a mercantile career in the Quaker city. Undaunted by his experiences, he made repeated voyages to Jamaica and other colonies, establishing connections and expanding his trading activities. He imported a great variety of manufactured goods from England: clothing and dress goods; gunpowder, shot, and nails; rugs and beaver hats. From the West Indies he brought in and sold molasses, rum, and sugar; spices; mahogany and other tropical woods. In turn he exported flour, bread, and biscuit; deerskins, tobacco, and any other Pennsylvania products for which he could find a market. In time he became one of Philadelphia's most active and prosperous merchants.

Nor did he neglect public service. For three years he was clerk of the Pennsylvania Assembly; later he was elected a member, and in 1718 he served as speaker. As one of the commissioners of streets and watercourses for the city, he was active in paving roadways, clearing docks, and improving landing places and bridges. From 1701 to 1711 he was a member of the Philadelphia Board of Aldermen and from 1712 to 1713 and again from 1717 to 1719 he was mayor of the city. From 1711 until his death eleven years later he served also as a member of the Provincial Council of Pennsylvania. The infant Jonathan, who almost miraculously survived the rigors of the shipwreck and its aftermath, was joined in time by two younger brothers, Joseph and John, and by two sisters, Mary and Hannah. Of these five children only the youngest, Hannah, had children of her own, so there have been no descendants of the Dickinson name to perpetuate their ancestor's memory. Jonathan Dickinson died in Philadelphia, June 11, 1722, at the age of fifty-nine, one of the city's most respected citizens.

Nature and man have combined to change greatly the region through which the *Reformation* party traveled so painfully more than two and a half centuries ago. Storms and ocean currents have shifted or closed some of the inlets they crossed on the long island chain up the Florida coast and changed the beaches in many places. Dredging and other improvements along the Intracoastal Waterway have transformed some of the passages their canoes negotiated with such difficulty into a yachtsman's highway. Most striking of all, the entire coastal reach from Jupiter Inlet north to the St. Mary's River and beyond has become part of a region of settled towns and cities and of vacation resorts where men and women come in thousands every year for rest and relaxation and a winter sojourn in the sunshine. Dickinson and his companions would be lost in wonder if they could revisit today the scene of their hard-ships long ago.

Any attempt to reconstruct on the grounds the itinerary of that journey of the distant past must take into account these changes that have taken place. But if some sturdy individual of our time should undertake to repeat, partly on foot and partly by canoe or open boat, the trip that Dickinson took, starting at the same time of year and spending the same calendar days in moving from place to place, this is approximately what he would do and these are the modern names of some places he would pass along the way:

Our man may well decide to prepare for the expedition at Palm Beach and then travel north by any suitable conveyance along Route U.S. 1 about seventeen miles to the south side of Jupiter Inlet. If he arrives on September 25, the same day that the *Reformation* castaways did (though they came from the scene of the wreck five miles north on Jupiter Island), he has three days to spend at the site of the first Indian village where they stayed. He has time for a quick visit to a place of particular interest to him only a few miles away, but perhaps he will appreciate it even more if he waits to do so until he comes back from the north. On September 28 he crosses the inlet and starts out. He camps out on the south side of St. Lucie Inlet the night of the 29th, too far away to see the town of Stuart a short distance up the St. Lucie River but close enough to sense the presence in the neighborhood of a much more friendly people than Dickinson was to meet in that vicinity. Crossing the inlet the next morning, he stops for two days and a night at the site of an Indian village a short distance north on Hobe Island, and sets out again on the evening of October 1.

After walking all night our man passes, soon after sunrise, the spot where the bark *Nantwich* was wrecked—the other ill-fated vessel in the convoy from Jamaica—and a mile or so further on he crosses Fort Pierce Inlet. For the moment he has no time to visit the present town of Fort Pierce over on the mainland but presses on till he reaches the site of the Indian village of Jece, on the river side of the island, not far from

Vero Beach. The man who is following Dickinson's itinerary is privileged to stay here a whole month, though he will not now have to find shelter in a primitive Indian hut, or move from hut to hut as violent storms flood the village, or try to keep out the increasing chill of autumn with only a few rags of clothing. And it is to be hoped that his food supply is tastier and more adequate than that of the Dickinson party.

Although some members of the combined groups of *Reformation* and *Nantwich* survivors left Jece on November 2, our man, following Dickinson's own movements, stays on until the 5th, when he sets out by water, moving north along the river. Without stopping to visit Melbourne on the mainland or any of the island beaches along the way, he reaches the region behind Cape Canaveral, now easily traversed by the Intracoastal Waterway but then a maze of creeks, marshy islands, and difficult passages which required three days, November 7 to 9, for Dickinson to negotiate. Our modern voyager, less preoccupied with the sheer labor of travel than Dickinson was, has time here to reflect on the great changes that have come to all our civilization in this long span of time, and especially in very recent years, symbolized with particular vividness by the activities now taking place at the Missile Test Base to the east of the Waterway on the cape.

Pushing on up the Indian River (or Mosquito) Lagoon the modern traveler passes New Smyrna Beach and crosses Ponce de Leon Inlet on November 11. The same day he passes through Daytona Beach along the Halifax River. The weather should be getting much colder now, the northwest wind blowing violently, and our man, himself well clothed, draws on his imagination to appreciate the suffering that the almost naked castaways must have experienced here. On November 13, leaving his boat at some point near Ormond Beach or Tomoka State Park and walking along the shore, he pictures to himself the horror of that day in 1696. As he passes Flagler and Beverly Beaches he must remember that several of the *Reformation* party had reached the limits of endurance. Five of the group died that day, somewhere along this shore, before they could reach the comparative safety of the first Spanish sentinel's house, located very near to where the tourist mecca of Marineland now stands. Moving on the next morning through deep sand, the traveler crosses Matanzas Inlet three or four miles to the north, passing the site of another sentinel's house and stopping for the night at a third. The final stage of the journey brings him at last to St. Augustine, November 15, about 230 miles from his starting point.

If our twentieth-century adventurer is still eager to follow Dickinson's route all the way to Charleston, he will have to go most of the way by water, and as he passes among the islands of the Georgia and South Carolina coast he will have fewer certain landmarks with which to plan and time his journey, for Dickinson's descriptions of the passages and creeks through which he moved are often too vague for precise identification. If, however, our man is determined to go on, he leaves St. Augustine on November 29 and spends that night on the site of the Indian village of St. Croix ("St. Cruce") and the next at a spot where once stood a Spanish sentinel's house. He reaches the site of the Indian town and Spanish mission of St. Juan ("St. Wans"), close to the present Fort Caroline National Monument, on December 1. Crossing Fort George Inlet the next morning, but not detouring up the St. John's River to Jacksonville, he travels along the coast past Fort Clinch to St. Mary's before sunset, and remains there until the 6th. During the next eight days he rows northward through Georgia waters, threading his way among the islands, and reaching St. Catherine Sound on the 14th. Then he crosses the mouth of the Savannah River into South Carolina, and passes through Port Royal Sound on the 21st. Taking one of the inland passages to St. Helen Sound, he reaches the site of Richard Bennet's plantation—in 1696 the southernmost English-speaking settlement—on the 22nd, then turns into the Combahee River, the South Edisto, and the Wadalow, and arrives at the Stono River and the site of Governor Blake's plantation the next day. He finally reaches Charleston the day after Christmas.

Our voyager has one great satisfaction yet in store, which he will now especially appreciate if he has saved it, as suggested earlier, until he returns to southern Florida from this long journey. When he reaches Stuart on the St. Lucie River while on his way back to Palm Beach, he must be sure to drive thirteen miles south on Route U.S. 1 and visit Jonathan Dickinson State Park, named in memory of the man whose passage up the coast he has been repeating. This tract of about 10,000 acres was the site of Camp Murphy, a radar training base in World War II, and has since been taken over by the State of Florida as a place for camping, boating, and general relaxation and communion with nature in one of its kindliest moods. Bordered on the west by the beautiful Loxahatchee River and the quiet Kitchen's Creek, it is a peaceful haven from the noise and strains of modern civilization. Wild life abounds here, lakes and streams add to its attractiveness, and the whole area attests to the charm that unspoiled nature alone can provide. If Jonathan Dickinson could visit the scene of his shipwreck again he would certainly be pleased that this park, only a few miles from the spot where he was cast away, is named in his honor, and that its quiet beauty invites the wayfarer to such rest and recreation as none of the *Reformation's* survivors could experience on this coast so long ago.

We do not know just when and how Dickinson wrote this account. It has the form of a daily record, although there are no entries for a little more than a third of the days between the shipwreck and the arrival of the survivors at Charleston. Any journal he might have kept during the voyage must have been lost when he got ashore, and of course neither he nor any other member of the group could have written down any sort of daily record between that time and their arrival at St. Augustine. Nor is it likely that he attempted any systematic writing during the voyage by open boat from St. Augustine to Charleston. The party spent about a month at the Indian town of Jece and two weeks at St. Augustine; several of the group remained at Charleston for nearly three months before sailing for Philadelphia. So there must have been many opportunities during these intervals between periods of daily movement and constant exposure for them to talk over their individual experiences and to refresh each other's memories as to the exact sequence of events. While the party was resting at St. Augustine the governor and two of his officers examined the castaways in great detail and had them sign the resulting statement.

Dickinson may have taken a copy of this document with him to Philadelphia, but whether he did or not, it is clear that when he came to write down the "journal" which has come down to us, probably only after he reached the peaceful Quaker city, he had the details of the whole journey so firmly fixed in mind that he could compose his narrative in the form of a day-by-day record, omitting only those days on which nothing had occurred which seemed worth mentioning. To substantiate the correctness of the account, the Quaker leaders responsible for its publication showed the manuscript to Joseph Kirle, former master of the *Reformation,* who read it and gave it his approval before it went to press. We can feel confident that in all important respects Dickinson's journal is an accurate account of what happened to him and his fellow travelers.

There was no printing press in Philadelphia when the *Reformation* party arrived; William Bradford the elder, Pennsylvania's first printer, had run into difficulties with the Quakers and had moved to New York four years before, taking his press and equipment with him. The Quaker Yearly Meeting tried to get a new press from England and someone to run it, but they did not succeed in either respect until the very end of 1698 when a second-hand press and a meager supply of badly worn type arrived. The printer they engaged after some searching was not much more promising than the equipment he was expected to use. Reiner Jansen was a Dutchman who had been converted to Quakerism and whom William Penn had persuaded to migrate to Pennsylvania. He arrived in 1698 with four of his five children. He had been a lace maker in the Netherlands and was now interested in farming, but he did not stay long on the twenty-acre piece of land he bought in Germantown; instead he moved to Philadelphia in 1699 to become a merchant. At some period in his earlier career he had picked up a little experience as a printer, and although the Quakers had misgivings about his qualifications, they could find no one better suited and they put him in charge of the press. Dickinson's journal was the first manuscript they gave him to print; the book, a deplorable example of crude typography, appeared in August 1699.

In addition to the Jansen edition, of which six copies are known to survive, there exists a manuscript copy, probably contemporary, written in an unknown hand, which one of Solomon Cresson's descendants acquired from a former owner about a century and a half later and gave to the Historical Society of Pennsylvania in 1877. And since the first publication of 1699 there has been a total of twenty-two reprintings in English, Dutch, and German, not including the thoroughly edited version of 1945 prepared by Evangeline W. and Charles M. Andrews upon which the present publication is based. In both the 1945 edition and this one the text of the journal is taken from Jansen's first printing of 1699, but with his spelling, capitalization, and punctuation modernized and his almost countless typographical errors silently corrected.

True to their deeply religious natures, the Quaker publishers of the book gave it the title *God's Protecting Providence Man's Surest Help and Defence In the times Of the greatest difficulty and most Imminent danger.* Through most of its history the work has been known more simply as *God's Protecting Providence.* Some one of the Philadelphia Friends also provided an extensive Preface, which, not being a part of Dickinson's narrative, is here reprinted in the appendix. Drawing pointed religious lessons from the experiences of the castaways and dwelling at length on Robert Barrow's edifying life and final hours, this composition's tone of pious moralizing suggests what the chief values were that its sponsors found in Dickinson's manuscript. Some present-day readers may agree with this judgment; others with a more secular approach will find different reasons for their interest. In either case, all should agree that this journal is a memorable account of hardship and suffering bravely borne, and of a stirring episode from America's early years.

At St. Lucie's.

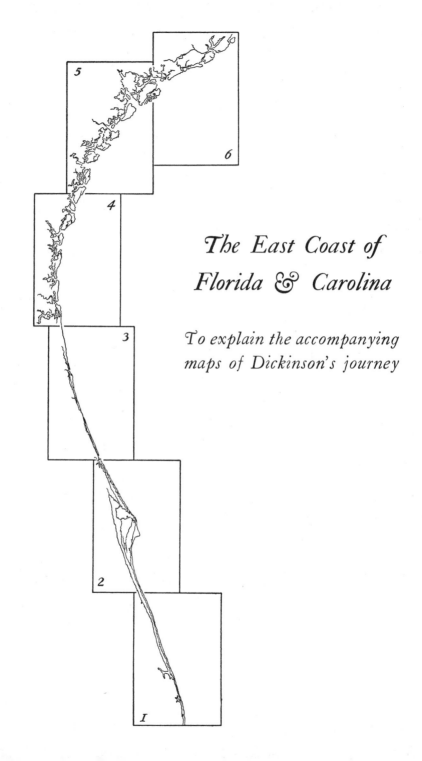

The East Coast of
Florida & Carolina

To explain the accompanying
maps of Dickinson's journey

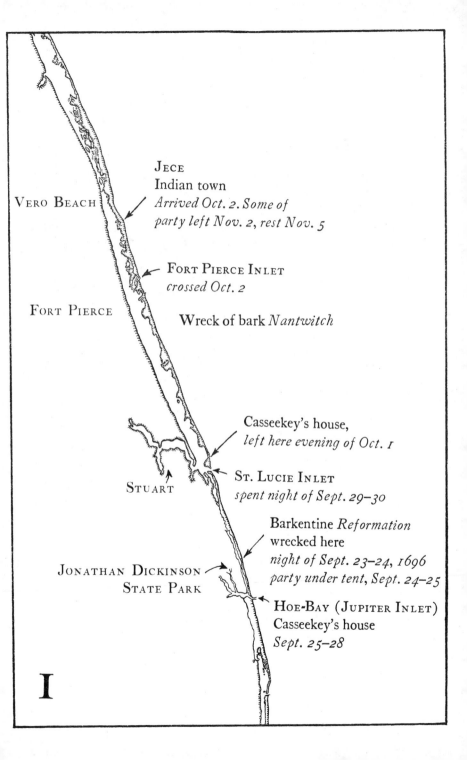

VERO BEACH

JECE
Indian town
*Arrived Oct. 2. Some of
party left Nov. 2, rest Nov. 5*

FORT PIERCE INLET
crossed Oct. 2

FORT PIERCE

Wreck of bark *Nantwitch*

Casseekey's house,
left here evening of Oct. 1

St. LUCIE INLET
spent night of Sept. 29–30

STUART

Barkentine *Reformation*
wrecked here
*night of Sept. 23–24, 1696
party under tent, Sept. 24–25*

JONATHAN DICKINSON
STATE PARK

HOE-BAY (JUPITER INLET)
Casseekey's house
Sept. 25–28

I

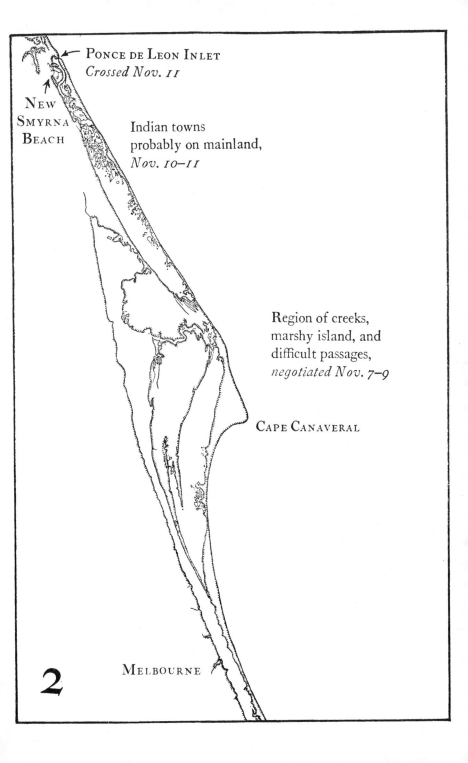

PONCE DE LEON INLET
Crossed Nov. 11

NEW
SMYRNA
BEACH

Indian towns
probably on mainland,
Nov. 10–11

Region of creeks,
marshy island, and
difficult passages,
negotiated Nov. 7–9

CAPE CANAVERAL

2

MELBOURNE

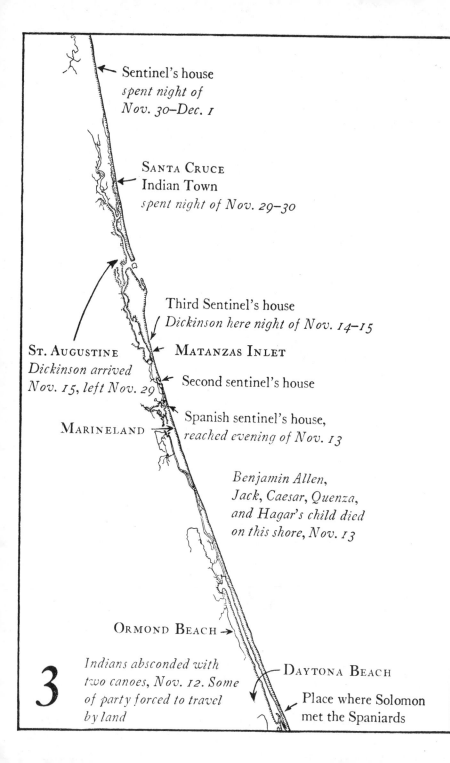

Sentinel's house
*spent night of
Nov. 30–Dec. 1*

SANTA CRUCE
Indian Town
spent night of Nov. 29–30

Third Sentinel's house
Dickinson here night of Nov. 14–15

ST. AUGUSTINE
*Dickinson arrived
Nov. 15, left Nov. 29*

MATANZAS INLET

Second sentinel's house

MARINELAND

Spanish sentinel's house,
reached evening of Nov. 13

*Benjamin Allen,
Jack, Caesar, Quenza,
and Hagar's child died
on this shore, Nov. 13*

ORMOND BEACH →

3

*Indians absconded with
two canoes, Nov. 12. Some
of party forced to travel
by land*

← DAYTONA BEACH

Place where Solomon
met the Spaniards

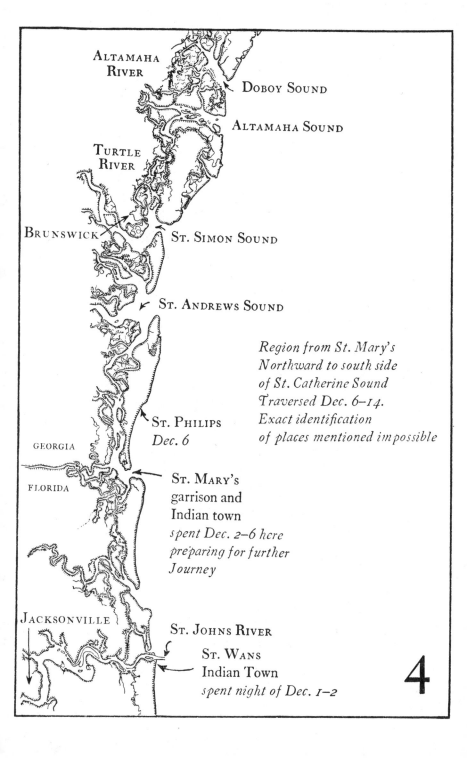

ALTAMAHA
RIVER

DOBOY SOUND

ALTAMAHA SOUND

TURTLE
RIVER

BRUNSWICK

ST. SIMON SOUND

ST. ANDREWS SOUND

*Region from St. Mary's
Northward to south side
of St. Catherine Sound
Traversed Dec. 6–14.
Exact identification
of places mentioned impossible*

ST. PHILIPS
Dec. 6

GEORGIA

FLORIDA

ST. MARY'S
garrison and
Indian town
*spent Dec. 2–6 here
preparing for further
Journey*

JACKSONVILLE

ST. JOHNS RIVER

ST. WANS
Indian Town
spent night of Dec. 1–2

4

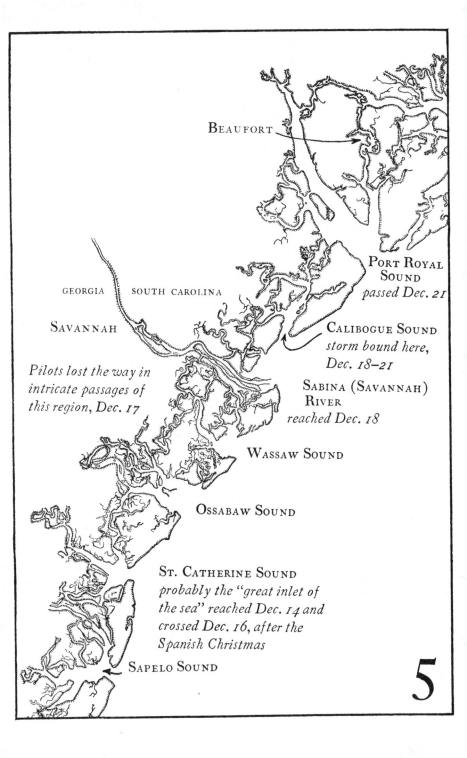

BEAUFORT

PORT ROYAL SOUND
passed Dec. 21

GEORGIA   SOUTH CAROLINA

SAVANNAH

CALIBOGUE SOUND
*storm bound here,
Dec. 18–21*

SABINA (SAVANNAH)
RIVER
reached Dec. 18

*Pilots lost the way in
intricate passages of
this region, Dec. 17*

WASSAW SOUND

OSSABAW SOUND

ST. CATHERINE SOUND
*probably the "great inlet of
the sea" reached Dec. 14 and
crossed Dec. 16, after the
Spanish Christmas*

SAPELO SOUND

5

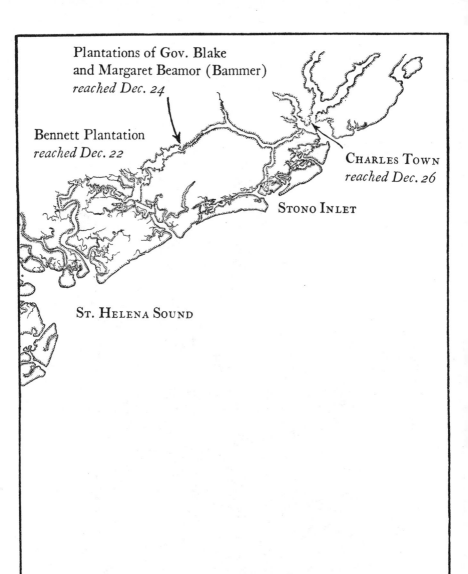

Plantations of Gov. Blake
and Margaret Beamor (Bammer)
reached Dec. 24

Bennett Plantation
reached Dec. 22

CHARLES TOWN
reached Dec. 26

STONO INLET

ST. HELENA SOUND

6

Arrival at St. Augustine.

GODS

PROTECTING PROVIDENCE
MAN'S
SUREST HELP AND DEFENCE

In the times
Of the greateſt difficulty and moſt Imminent danger;
Evidenced in the

Remarkable Deliverance

Of divers Perſons,
From the devouring Waves of the Sea, amongſt which
they Suffered Shipwrack.
And alſo
From the more cruelly devouring jawes of the inhumane
CANIBALS of FLORIDA.
Faithfully related by one of the perſons concerned therein;
JONATHAN DICKENSON.

Psal. 93 : 4. *The Lord on high is mightier than the noiſe of many Waters,
yea than the mighty Waves of the Sea.*
Psal. 74 : 20. *The dark places of the Earth are full of the habitations
of Cruelty.*

Printed in *Philadelphia* by *Reinier Janſen.* 1699.

A Journal

of the Travels of Several Persons, with their Sufferings, Being Cast Away in the Gulf (amongst the Cannibals) of Florida. &c.

Persons' Names viz.

Joseph Kirle Commander of the Barkentine, *Reformation.*

Richard Limpeney Mate.
Solomon Cresson.
Joseph Buckley.
Thomas Fownes.
Thomas Jemmet. } Mariners.
Nathaniel Randall.
John Hilliard, the Master's Boy.
Ben, the Master's Negro.

Robert Barrow.
Jonathan Dickinson.
Mary Dickinson. } Passengers.
Jonathan Dickinson, a sucking Child six months old.
Benjamin Allen.

Peter.
London.
Jack. } Negro Men.
Cesar.
Cajoe, a Child.
} Belonging to *Jonathan Dickinson.*
Hagar.
Sarah.
Bella. } Negro Women.
Susanna.
Quensa.

Venus, an Indian Girl.

2

The twenty-third day of the sixth month called August 1696. Being in company with twelve or thirteen sail of merchant-men under the convoy of the *Hampshire* Frigate, Captain Fletcher commander, sailed from Port Royal in Jamaica, we being bound for Pennsylvania.

*The 6 Month, 24; the 2 day of the week.**
This day about noon came a sloop from Port Royal, meeting us off Portland; gave an account of the French fleet's being at Cape Antonio.

This evening we lay by off Black River's mouth in order to go the next morning to Bluefield, but it being calm for many days following, the current drove to westward of the island.

The 6 Month, 31; the 2 day of the week.
This evening we lost sight of the *Hampshire* Frigate, and then beat to windward again.

The 7 Month, 1; the 3 day of the week.
This evening we anchored to westward of Savanna La Mar, and lost our anchor.

The 7 Month, 2; the 4 day of the week.
This day we got in Bluefield Road to water.

The 7 Month, 4; the 6 day of the week.
This morning we sailed from Bluefields intending our passage through the Gulf.

The 7 Month, 14; the 2 day of the week.
This day about noon were abreast with Cape Antonio and about a league to the eastwards of the cape was a fire, making a great smoke. At length people appeared on the bay, making signs for us to put on shore; but having a fresh gale and not knowing who they were, our master would not.

This day made the tableland of the Havana and this eve-

* From the beginning through the heading for 7 Month 29 Day (September 29) the 1699 edition gives the day of the month and of the week as columnar entries in the left-hand margin of the page. In the present printing they have been transcribed into the heading form which the printer of the 1699 edition used regularly after these first entries.

ning stood over for Cape Florida; but about eight or nine at night we saw two lights, being about a mile from us: we fearing we were got amongst the French fleet, tacked and stood for the Havana.

The 7 Month, 18; the 6 day of the week.

This morning no sail appeared and being most of the day calm we lay about four leagues off the Havana; had we had a fair wind were designed for that port to inquire of the French fleet. This afternoon came a tornado from the land; and our master being on the quarterdeck, our boom jibing knocked him down and broke his leg: which accident was grievous to him and us; but I having things suitable, with a little experience set it. At this time had I four of my family very sick, one whereof was an Indian girl being, just as I had bound up the master's leg, taken with fits which continued some hours and then she died. This evening we stood over for Cape Florida, having the wind northeasterly.

The 7 Month, 19; the 7 day of the week.

This morning the wind not being fair, we stood up for Cuba, and about sun-rising we espied the two sail that we saw before, they standing as we stood. Therefore we supposed them to be some of our company. We wronged them in sailing, and by noon lost sight of them. About four this afternoon we espied a ship to the eastward of us (we being about four leagues off shore and about fifteen leagues to eastward of the Havana) supposing her to be a Frenchman, therefore stood in for the shore, but she gained on us: when a tornado sprang up and a great shower of rain followed which hid us; hereupon we tacked and stood over for Florida. Night came on that we saw no more of that sail, having the wind fair.

The 7 Month, 20; the 1 day of the week.

This morning were in the gulf, having a fair wind, and seeing the two ships following us, we believed them to be of our company.

The 7 Month, 21; the 2 day of the week.
This morning the wind at east and shifting northerly.

The 7 Month, 22; the 3 day of the week.
This day the storm began at N.E.

*The 7 Month, 23; the 4 day of the week.**
About one o'clock in the morning we felt our vessel strike
some few strokes, and then she floated again for five or six
minutes before she ran fast aground, where she beat violently
at first. The wind was violent and it was very dark, that our
mariners could see no land; the seas broke over us that we were
in a quarter of an hour floating in the cabin: we endeavored to
get a candle lighted, which in a little time was accomplished.
By this time we felt the vessel not to strike so often but several of her timbers were broken and some plank started. The
seas continued breaking over us and no land to be seen; we
concluded to keep in the vessel as long as she would hold together. About the third hour this morning we supposed we saw
the land at some considerable distance, and at this time we
found the water began to run out of the vessel. And at daylight we perceived we were upon the shore, on a beach lying in
the breach of the sea which at times as the surges of the sea re-
versed was dry. In taking a view of our vessel, we found that
the violence of the weather had forced many sorts of the sea-
birds on board of our vessel, some of which were by force of
the wind blown into and under our hen-cubs and many remained alive. Our hogs and sheep were washed away and
swam on shore, except one of the hogs which remained in the
vessel. We rejoiced at this our preservation from the raging
seas; but at the same instant feared the sad consequences that
followed: yet having hopes still we got our sick and lame on
shore, also our provisions, with spars and sails to make a tent.
I went with one Negro to view the land and seek the most con-

* The MS. copy leaves a blank after this date and gives the account of the
wreck, which here follows, under date of the 24th, 5th day of the week. It will
be noticed that the text below (following the printed edition of 1699) omits all
reference to 7 Month, 24 Day.

venient place for that purpose; but the wilderness country looked very dismal, having no trees, but only sand hills covered with shrubby palmetto, the stalks of which were prickly, that there was no walking amongst them. I espied a place almost a furlong within that beach being a bottom; to this place I with my Negro soon cut a passage, the storm and rain continuing. Thither I got my wife and sick child being six months and twelve days old, also Robert Barrow an aged man, who had been sick about five or six months, our master, who some days past broke his leg, and my kinsman Benjamin Allen, who had been very ill with a violent fever most part of the voyage: these with others we got to the place under the shelter of some few bushes which broke some of the wind, but kept none of the rain from them; I got a fire made. The most of our people were getting provisions ashore; our chests, trunks and the rest of our clothing were all very wet and cold.

About the eighth or ninth hour came two Indian men (being naked except a small piece of platted work of straws which just hid their private parts, and fastened behind with a horsetail in likeness made of a sort of silk-grass) from the southward, running fiercely and foaming at the mouth having no weapons except their knives: and forthwith not making any stop; violently seized the two first of our men they met with who were carrying corn from the vessel to the top of the bank, where I stood to receive it and put it into a cask. They used no violence for the men resisted not, but taking them under the arm brought them towards me. Their countenance was very furious and bloody. They had their hair tied in a roll behind in which stuck two bones shaped one like a broad arrow, the other a spearhead. The rest of our men followed from the vessel, asking me what they should do whether they should get their guns to kill these two; but I persuaded them otherwise desiring them to be quiet, showing their inability to defend us from what would follow; but to put our trust in the Lord who was able to defend to the uttermost. I walked towards the place where our sick and lame were, the two Indian men following me. I told them the Indians were come and coming upon us. And while these two (letting the men loose) stood with a wild, furious countenance, looking upon us I bethought myself to give them some tobacco and pipes, which they greedily snatched from me, and making a snuffing noise like a wild beast, turned their backs upon us and run away.

We communed together and considered our condition, being amongst a barbarous people such as were generally accounted man-eaters, believing those two were gone to alarm their people. We sat ourselves down, expecting cruelty and hard death, except it should please the Almighty God to work wonderfully for our deliverance. In this deep concernment some of us were not left without hopes; blessed be the name of the Lord in Whom we trusted.

As we were under a deep exercise and concernment, a motion arose from one of us that if we should put ourselves under the denomination of the Spaniards (it being known that that nation had some influence on them) and one of us named Solomon Cresson speaking the Spanish language well, it was hoped this might be a means for our delivery, to which the most of the company assented.

Within two or three hours after the departure of the two Indians, some of our people being near the beach or strand returned and said the Indians were coming in a very great number all running and shouting. About this time the storm was much abated, the rain ceased, and the sun appeared which had been hid from us many days. The Indians went all to the vessel, taking forth whatever they could lay hold on, except rum, sugar, molasses, beef and pork.

But their Casseekey (for so they call their king) with about thirty more came down to us in a furious manner, having a dismal aspect and foaming at the mouth. Their weapons were large Spanish knives, except their Casseekey's who had a bagganet that belonged to the master of our vessel: they rushed in upon us and cried *Nickaleer Nickaleer*. We understood them not at first: they repeating it over unto us often. At last they cried *Epainia* or *Spaniard*, by which we understood them that at first they meant *English;* but they were answered to the latter in Spanish yea to which they replied, *No Spainia No*, but all cried out, *Nickaleer, Nickaleer*. We sitting on our chests, boxes and trunks, and some on the ground, the Indians surrounded us. We stirred nor moved not; but sat all or most of us very calm and still, some of us in a good frame of spirit, being freely given up to the will of God.

Whilst we were thus sitting, as a people almost unconcerned, these bloody minded creatures placed themselves each behind one kicking and throwing away the bushes that were nigh or under their feet; the Casseekey had placed himself behind me, standing on the chest which I sat upon, they all having their arms extended with their knives in their hands, ready to execute their bloody design, some taking hold of some of us by the heads with their knees set against our shoulders. In this posture they seemed to wait for the Casseekey to begin. They were high in words which we understood not. But on a sudden it pleased the Lord to work wonderfully for our preservation, and instantly all these savage men were struck dumb, and like men amazed the space of a quarter of an hour, in which time their countenances fell, and they looked like another people. They quitted their places they had taken behind us, and came in amongst us requiring to have all our chests, trunks and boxes unlocked; which being done, they divided all that was in them. Our money the Casseekey took unto himself, privately hiding in the bushes. Then they went to pulling off our clothes, leaving each of us only a pair of breeches, or an old coat, except my wife and child, Robert Barrow and our master, from whom they took but little this day.

Having thus done, they asked us again, *Nickaleer, Nickaleer?* But we answered by saying *Pennsylvania*.

We began to enquire after St. Augustine, also would talk of St. Lucie,* which was a town that lay about a degree to the northward. But they cunningly would seem to persuade us that they both lay to the southward. We signified to them that they lay to the northward. And we would talk of the Havana

---

* Spelled throughout the 1699 edition "St. a Lucea."

that lay to the southward. These places they had heard of and knew which way they lay.

At length the Casseekey told us how long it was to St. Lucie by days' travel; but cared not to hear us mention St. Augustine. They would signify by signs we should go to the southward. We answered that we must go to the northward for Augustine. When they found they could not otherwise persuade us, they signified that we should go to the southward for the Havana, and that it was but a little way.

We gave them to understand that we came that way and were for the northward; all which took place with them. We perceived that the Casseekey's heart was tendered towards us; for he kept mostly with us and would the remaining part of this day keep off the petty robbers which would have had our few rags from us. Sometime before night we had a shower of rain, whereupon the Casseekey made signs for us to build some shelter; upon which we got our tent up and some leaves to lie upon.

About this time our vessel lay dry on shore and the Indians gathered themselves together men and women, some hundreds in numbers. Having got all the goods out of the vessel and covered the bay for a large distance, opened all the stuffs and linens and spread them to dry, they would touch no sort of strong drink, sugar, nor molasses, but left it in the vessel. They shouted and made great noises in the time of plunder. Night coming on the Casseekey put those chests and trunks which he had reserved for himself into our tent; which pleased us, and gave an expectation of his company for he was now become a defender of us from the rage of others. The Casseekey went down to the waterside amongst his people and returned with three old coats that were wet and torn, which he gave us; one whereof I had. We made a fire at each end of our tent and laid ourselves down, it being dark: but hearing hideous noises and fearing that they were not satisfied, we expected them upon us. The chief Indian (or Casseekey) lay in the tent upon his chests. And about midnight we heard a company of Indians coming from the vessel towards us, making

terrible shouts, and coming fiercely up to the tent, the Casseekey called to them; which caused them to stand. It seemed,
they had killed a hog and brought him: So the Casseekey
asked us, if we would eat the hog? Solomon Cresson, by our
desire answered him, that we used not to eat at that time of
the night: whereupon they threw the hog down before the
tent, and the Casseekey sent them away. They went shouting
to the sea-shore, where there were some hundreds of them
revelling about our wreck.

The 7 month, 25; the 6 day of the week.

This morning having purposed to endeavor for liberty to
pass to the northward, Solomon opened the matter to the Casseekey; who answered we must go to his town to the southward.

This occasioned us to press him more urgently to let us go to
St. Lucie (this place having a Spanish name supposed to have
found it under the government of that nation, whence we
might expect relief). But the Casseekey told us that it was
about two or three days' journey thither and that when we
came there, we should have our throats and scalps cut and be
shot, burnt and eaten. We thought that information was but
to divert us; so that we were more earnest to go but he sternly
denied us, saying, we must go to his town.

About eight o'clock this morning the Casseekey came into
our tent and set himself amongst us, asking the old question,
Nickaleer, Nickaleer? directing his speech to one particular
of us, who in simplicity answered, yes. Which caused the Casseekey to ask the said person, if another person which he
pointed to, was *Nickaleer?* He answered, yes. Then he said,
Totus (or all) *Nickaleer*, and went from amongst us. Returning in a short time with some of his men with him, and afresh
they went greedily to stripping my wife and child, Robert
Barrow and our master who had escaped it till now. Thus
were we left almost naked, till the feud was something abated
and then we got somewhat from them which displeased some
of them. We then cut our tents in pieces, and got the most of

our clothing out of it: which the Indians perceiving, took the remains from us. We men had most of us breeches and pieces of canvas, and all our company interceded for my wife that all was not taken from her. About noon the Indians having removed all their plunder off the bay, and many of them gone, a guard was provided armed with bows and arrows, with whom we were summoned to march and a burden provided for everyone to carry that was any ways able. Our master with his broken leg was helped along by his Negro Ben. My wife was forced to carry her child, they not suffering any of us to relieve her. But if any of us offered to lay down our burden, we were threatened to be shot. Thus were we forced along the beach bare-footed.

We had saved one of the master's quadrants, and seamen's calendar, with two other books. As we walked along the bay (the time suiting) our mate Richard Limpeney took an observation, and we found ourselves to be in the latitude of twenty-seven degrees and eight minutes. Some of the Indians were offended at it: when he held up his quadrant to observe, one would draw an arrow to shoot him; but it pleased God hitherto to prevent them from shedding any of our blood.

One passage I have omitted. Two of our mariners named Thomas Fownes and Richard Limpeney went forth this morning from our tent down to the bay where the Indians were, and viewing of them at some distance, an Indian man came running upon them, with his knife in his hand, and took hold of Thomas Fownes to stab him; but the said Thomas fell on his knees, using a Spanish ceremony, and begged not to kill him; whereupon the Indian desisted, and bid him be gone to the place from which he came. The said Thomas at his return acquainted us how narrowly he had escaped.

After we had traveled about five miles along the deep sand, the sun being extreme hot, we came to an inlet. On the other side was the Indian town, being little wigwams made of small poles stuck in the ground, which they bended one to another, making an arch, and covered them with thatch of small palmetto-leaves. Here we were commanded to sit down, and the Casseekey came to us, who with his hand scratched a hole in the sand about a foot deep, and came to water, which he made signs for us to come and drink. We, being extreme thirsty, did; but the water was almost salt. Whilst we sat here, we saw great fires making on the other side of the inlet, which some of us thought was preparing for us. After an hour's time being spent here at length came an Indian with a small canoe from the other side and I with my wife and child and Robert Barrow were ordered to go in. The same canoe was but just wide enough for us to sit down in. Over we were carried, and being landed, the man made signs for us to walk to the wigwams, which we did; but the young Indians would seem to be frighted and fly from us. We were directed to a wigwam, which afterwards we understood to be the Casseekey's. It was about man-high to the top. Herein was the Casseekey's wife and some old women sitting on a cabin made of sticks about a foot high covered with a mat; they made signs for us to sit down on the ground; which we did, the Casseekey's wife having a young child sucking at her breast gave it to another woman, and would have my child; which my wife was very loath to suffer; but she would not be denied, took our child and suckled it at her breast viewing and feeling it from top to toe; at length returned it to my wife, and by this time was another parcel of our people come over; and sitting down by the wigwam side our Indian brought a fish boiled on a small palmetto leaf and set it down amongst us, making signs for us to eat; but our exercise was too great for us to have any inclination to receive food. At length all our people were brought over, and afterwards came the Casseekey. As soon as he came to his wigwam he set himself to work, got some stakes and stuck them in a row joining to his wigwam and tied some sticks whereon were these small palmettos, tied and fastened them to the stakes about three foot high; and laid two or three mats made of reeds down by this shelter; which, it seems, he made for us to break the wind off us; and ordered us to lie down there; which we did, as many as the mats would hold; the rest lay on the ground by us. The Casseekey went into his wigwam and seated himself on his cabin cross-legged having a basket of palmetto berries brought him, which he eat very greedily: after which came some Indians unto him and talked much. Night came on; the moon being up, an Indian, who performeth their ceremonies stood out, looking full at the moon making a hideous noise, and crying out acting like a mad man for the space of half an hour; all the Indians being silent till he had done: after which they all made fearful noise some like the barking of a dog, wolf, and other strange sounds. After this, one gets a log and sets himself down, holding the stick or log upright on the ground, and several others getting about him, made a hideous noise, singing to our amazement; at length their women joined consort, making the noise more terrible. This they continued till midnight. Towards morning was great dews: our fire being expended, we were extreme cold.

The 7 Month, 26; the 7 day of the week.
This morning the Casseekey looking on us with a mild aspect, sent his son with his striking staff to the inlet to strike fish for us; which was performed with great dexterity; for some of us walked down with him, and though we looked very earnestly when he threw his staff from him could not see a fish at which time he saw it, and brought it on shore on the end of his staff. Sometimes he would run swiftly pursuing a fish, and seldom missed when he darted at him. In two hours' time he got as many fish as would serve twenty men: there were others also fishing at the same time, so that fish was plenty: but the sense of our conditions stayed our hungry stomachs: for some amongst us thought they would feed us to feed themselves.

The Casseekey went this morning towards our vessel; in his absence the other Indians looked very untowardly upon us, which created a jealousy of their cruelty yet to come.

This afternoon we saw a great fire nigh the place of our vessel; whereupon we concluded that our vessel and our boat were burnt: whereupon we were almost confirmed that they designed to destroy us. About sunsetting the Casseekey came home: we spake to him; he answered us and seemed very affable; which we liked well. Night drawing on and the wind shifting northward, we removed our shelter, and added the mats to it to break the wind off us, which blowed cold, and laid ourselves on the sand. About an hour within night came a parcel of Indians from the southward being all armed with bows and arrows and coming near our tent some of us espied them whereupon they squatted down. This seemed a fresh motive of danger, and we awakened those of us that were fallen asleep, and bid them prepare, for things seemed dangerous, we supposing they were come to forward our destruction or to carry us to the southward. They sat thus a considerable time; at length they distributed themselves to the wigwams. Thus would danger often appear unto us, and almost swallow us up; but at times we should be set over it, having a secret hope that God would work our deliverance, having preserved us from so many perils.

Sometime before night Robert Barrow was exhorting us to be patient and in a godly manner did he expound that text of scripture: *Because thou hast kept the word of my patience &c.* Rev., 3 Chap., 10 ver., after which he ended with a most fervent prayer desiring of the Lord that whereas He had suffered us to be cast amongst a barbarous and heathenish people, if that it was His blessed will, he would preserve and deliver us from amongst them, that our names might not be buried in oblivion; and that he might lay his body amongst faithful friends: and at the close of his prayer, he seemed to have an assurance that his petition would be granted. In all which some of us were livingly refreshed and strengthened.

The 7 month, 27; the 1 day of the week.
This morning we again used our endeavors with the Casseekey, that we might go to the northward for Augustine. His answer was, [we should go to the southward: for if we went to the northward,]* we should be all killed; but at length we prevailed, and he said, on the morrow we should go. Here-

---

* Here and similarly throughout, all words in brackets are found in the MS. copy but omitted in the Jansen printing of 1699.

upon he took three Negro men (one of Joseph Kirle's and two of mine) and with a canoe went up the sound.

This day the Indians were busy with what they had taken out of our vessel, and would have employed all of us to do, some one thing, some another for them; but we not knowing the consequence endeavored to shun it, and would deny their demands.

But some of our men did answer their desires in making and sewing some cloth together, stringing our beds, mending of locks, of the chests, &c. Whatever they thought was amiss they would be putting upon us to mend, still we wholly refused. At which time I heard a saying that came from one of the chief Indians, thus *"English Son of a Bitch,"* which words startled me; for I do believe they had had some of our nation in their possession, of whom they had heard such an expression: I passed away from the wigwam with much trouble.

This day being the first day of the week, we having a large Bible and a book of Robert Barclay's, some one or other was often reading in them. But being most of us sat together, Robert Barrow desired our people to wait upon the Lord: in which time Robert had a word in season unto us, and afterwards went to prayer, all the Indians coming about us, and some younger sort would be mocking; but not to our disturbance. The elder sort stood very modestly the whole time. After prayer ended, they all withdrew quietly: but some of them (especially the Casseekey's eldest son) would take great delight in our reading, and would take the Bible or other book, and give to one or other to read; the sound of which pleased them, for they would sit quietly and very attentively to hear us.

The Casseekey having been gone most part of the day with three Negroes (about the third hour in the afternoon we saw two of our Negroes) in our boat coming over the bar into the inlet. We rejoiced to see our boat, for we thought she had been burnt. Our Negroes told us, they went up sound with the Casseekey and landed near the place where our tent had been: the chief business was to remove the money from one place to another, and bury it. This old man would trust our people, but not his own. After that was done, they went to the place where our vessel was burnt; they launched our boat, in which the old Casseekey put his chests, wherein was our linen and other of our trade: also they got a small rundlet which they filled with wine out of a quarter cask that was left and brought sugar out of the wreck which was not consumed with the fire. But this time came the Casseekey and other Negro in the canoe. He told us, on the morrow we should go with our boat: this was cheerful news unto us. All the time some Indians had been out, and brought home some oysters, and the Casseekey gave us some, bidding us take what we had a mind to. A little before night* the Casseekey opened his chests and boxes; and his wife came and took what was in them from him: but he seemed very generous to my wife and child, and gave her several things which were useful to her and our child.

Our boat was very leaky; so we got her into a creek to sink her, that the water might swell her.

The 7 month, 28; the 2 day of the week.

This morning we waited an opportunity to get leave to depart, which was granted us: whereupon we asked for such things as they did not make use of; viz. a great glass, wherein was five or six pound of butter; some sugar; the rundlet of wine: and some balls of chocolate: all which was granted us; also a bowl to heave water out of the boat. But the Casseekey would have a Negro boy of mine, named Caesar, to which I could not tell what to say; but he was resolved on it. We got down to the waterside, and sent all our people over that were to travel: and Joseph Kirle, Robert Barrow, I, my wife and child with two of our mariners went in the boat, and rowed along shore northwards; but the Casseekey would have us to have gone with our boat up the sound. We supposed the sound was a great river; and therefore were not willing to take his advice, having no knowledge; but his counsel was good, as we found afterwards; for the conveniency of passage.

---

* "Midnight" in MS. copy.

The Casseekey and some other Indians went with our people towards our wreck, we rowing along shore, and our boat very leaky, that one person had employ enough to heave out the water.

Just before we left the Indian town, several Indians were for taking the little clothes and rags we had got; but calling out to the Casseekey, he would cause them to let us alone.

Solomon Cresson was mightily in one Indian's favor, who would hardly stir from his wigwam, but Solomon must be with him, and go arm in arm; which Indian amongst his plunder had a morning gown, which he put on Solomon, and Solomon had worn it most of the time we were there; but when the time of our departure came an Indian unrobed him, and left only a pair of breeches, and seemed very angry.

It was high noon when we left our wreck (she being burnt down to her floor timbers which lay in the sand) we setting forward, some in the boat, the rest traveled along shore; and a little before sun-setting, our people came up with abundance of small fish that had been forced on shore, as we may suppose, by the storm that drove us ashore (they lying far from the water, being much tainted), covered the shore for nigh a mile in length: of which our people gathered as many as they could carry. About sun-setting we put on shore to refresh ourselves, and take a small respite; also to take my kinsman Benjamin Allen into our boat: for this afternoon in his travel he was taken with a fever and ague, and we had much trouble to get him along, he having been sick nigh unto death (being first taken the day before we left Bluefields Road) until about a week before we were cast away.

One of my Negroes had saved a tinder-box and flint, and we had reserved two knives, by which means we got a fire, though with much difficulty, for our tinder was bad, and all the wood salt-water-soaken: which being accomplished, we broiled all our fish, feeding heartily of some of them, and the rest we kept not knowing when we should be thus furnished again; for which some of us were truly thankful to the God of all our mercies.

Having a large fire many of us got under the lee of it, and others buried themselves in the sand, in hopes to get a little sleep, that we might be somewhat refreshed, and thereby be the better enabled some to travel and some to row the remaining part of the night: but the sand flies and the mosquitoes were so extreme thick that it was impossible. The moon shining, we launched our boat I and my wife and child, the master, Robert Barrow, my kinsman Allen, Solomon Cresson, Joseph Buckley and the master's Negro went in our boat; the rest traveled along shore. About midnight, or a little after, our people came by an Indian town; the Indians came out in a great number, but offered no violence more than endeavoring to take from them what little they had: but making some small resistance, the Indians were put by their purpose. They were very desirous to have us come on shore, and would hail us; but our people would have us keep off. We were got among a parcel [of] breakers, and so had much ado to get out to sea.

The 7 month, 29; the 3 day of the week.
This morning about sun-rising we stood in for the land, and looked out for our people, but could not see them, therefore we lay by for the space of two hours and at length saw them coming along with a great many Indians with them. When they came abreast with us, the Indians wafted us ashore; but we refused, perceiving they were wickedly bent; they would be ever and anon snatching one thing or another: at which time our people would point to us in the boat; but perceiving they could not get us ashore, in some few hours left them.

This day noon Joseph Kirle having his quadrant and calendar, took an observation, being in latitude 27 deg. 45 min. About one o'clock we saw two Indians with bows and arrows running to meet our people; who when they saw them, at first they made a halt and afterwards retreated: at which the Indians let fly an arrow; which narrowly escaped one of them. Whereupon they stopped; the Indians looked strangely on them; but our people set forwards, and the Indians with them until they came to the Indian town. We saw our people go into the wigwams, but stayed a very short time; for the Indians were for taking those pieces of canvas they had from them. They got some water and set forward again; the two Indians still followed them. About this time we saw a sail to the eastward, and we supposing it at first to be a brigantine, agreed to follow her; but in a small time we made it to be a canoe or boat with two masts and sails. She stood in for the shore; but as soon as they espied us she bore away: and when she saw we made not after her, she stood ashore again for the Indian town; hereupon a jealousy got amongst us that she might go on shore and get strong with men, and then come after us; whereupon we rowed very hard and kept an offing for some hours; but finding they came not out, we stood towards the shore again. This day was extreme hot and we had no water since we left the Indian town to the southward of our wreck, called by the name of Hoe-Bay; therefore we were desirous to get on shore, but when we endeavored it, we could not; for the seas swelling very much, and came rolling from the eastward: so that the seas run very hollow, and broke almost a mile from the shore. Our master said it was impossible to get on shore alive: but I being under some exercise was desirous to be on shore, and thereupon did express myself to the rest of our people; they stated the danger; all which I was as sensible of as they, yet I could not rest but insisted on going ashore. The master and men said we should not save our lives; but I gained so far, that they attempted and were got within half a mile of the shore; but the seas came on us so large and hollow that one sea had liked to have overwhelmed us: we just got atop of it before it broke. There was then no persuading them to go further, but we stood off, and designed to keep off all night, our people being very weary and the sun setting; we divided one half to get some sleep, the other to watch and keep the boat's head to the sea. The weather looked as though it would be bad, and the sea increased; whereupon I began afresh to persuade them to go on shore. All were desirous, but thought it impossible. At length we resolved to venture; and so committing ourselves to the protection of the Almighty God, we stood in for the shore, and made signs to our people that we designed it. And it pleased God to order it so that we went on shore, as though there had been a lane made through the breakers, and were carried to the top of the bank, where we got aged Robert Barrow, my wife and child out of the boat, before ever a sea came to fill us; which did, as soon as they were got out: but we got our boat up from the wash of the sea.

The two Indians were for taking off our clothes, (which would not cover our bodies) but we not being willing to yield, they would snatch a piece from one and a bit from another, and run away with that, and then come again and do the like. These two Indians took away what was given to my wife and child which we knew not how to help, but exercised patience.

We inquired how far it was from St. Lucie (one of them speaking a little Spanish) and by signs we understood it was not far. They made signs that when we came there we should be put to most cruel death but we hoped otherwise.

At this place within the land, and over the sound our people said, before it was dark, they saw two or three houses, which looked white, though they were plastered with lime; which put us in hopes that there were Spaniards there; so we set forward as the Indians directed for St. Lucie. They made signs that we should come to an inlet of the sea, and on the other side was St. Lucie. We traveled about four miles and came to the inlet, but saw no settlement on the other side; so we concluded to lie there all night. We saw the track of a large bear and other wild beasts; whereupon we set to work to get wood and then a fire. Abundance of mosquitoes and sand-flies hindered our rest, to remedy which we digged holes in the sand, got some grass and laid it therein to lie upon, in order to cover ourselves from the flies, which most of us did; but it being extreme cold, and firing scarce, we had little comfort.

About midnight we sent our people to see if they could get off our boat, and bring it into the inlet, that we might get over to the other side. They went and launched her, but the sea was so rough that there was no possibility of getting her off, for she was soon filled, and put to swim, and they, boat and all, were driven on shore again.

Whilst our people were gone for the boat, we espied some Indians in a canoe with their torch a-fishing: we sent for Solomon (who was gone to launch the boat) expecting they would come, seeing fires, and we should not tell what to say to them; but they did not. Here we lay watching, for no rest could be taken.

The 7 month, 30; the 2 day of the week.

This morning by break of day we saw a small canoe from the other side put off shore with two Indians, in her going up the river (or sound) a-fishing. We hailed them in Spanish, and as soon as they heard and saw us, they made to the shore with all speed, and away to their town they run. We perceiving they were shy of us, began to doubt of their amity which we had so much depended on; whereupon we counseled our people how to deport themselves, especially our Negroes. About sun-rising we saw the Indians coming, running in a very great number with their bows and arrows to the inlet; where having five or six canoes, they got into them as many as those canoes could hold. Others took the water, and swam over unto us; they came in the greatest rage that possibly a barbarous people could. Solomon began to speak Spanish to them; but they answered not, till they came ashore some distance from us; and then coming running upon us, they cried out, *Nickaleer, Nickaleer.* We sat all still expecting death, and that in a most barbarous manner. They that did speak unto them could not be heard: but they rushed violently on us rending and tearing those few clothes we had: they that had breeches had so many about them, that they hardly touched the ground till they were shaken out of them. They tore all from my wife, and espying her hair-lace, some were going to cut it hair and (all) away to get it, but, like greedy dogs, another snatched and tore it off. As for our poor young child, they snatched from it what little it had, as though they would have shaken and torn it, limb from limb. After they had taken all from us but our lives, they began to talk one to another, vehemently foaming at mouth, like wild boars, and taking their bows and arrows with other weapons, cried out *Nickaleer, Nickaleer*. Solomon spake in Spanish to them, and said we were Spaniards; but they would not hear him, and continued crying out *Nickaleer, Nickaleer*, withal drawing their arrows to the head. But suddenly we perceived them to look about and listen, and then desisted to prosecute their bloody design. One of them took a pair of breeches and gave it to my wife. We brought our great Bible and a large book of Robert Barclay's to this place. And being all stripped as naked as we were born, and endeavoring to hide our nakedness; these cannibals took the books, and tearing out the leaves would give each of us a leaf to cover us; which we took from them: at which time they would deride and smite us; and instantly another of them would snatch away what the other gave us, smiting and deriding us withal.

Robert Barrow with myself, wife and child were ordered to go in to a canoe to be carried to the other side of the inlet, being a furlong over, four Indians being in the canoe to paddle. When we came to the other side within a canoe's length or two of the shore, a number of Indians with their bows and arrows came running into the water, some to their knees, some deeper, having their bows and arrows drawn up, crying out *Nickaleer, Nickaleer;* which they continued without ceasing. The Indians that brought us over leaped out of the canoe, and swam ashore, fearing they should be shot; but in this juncture it pleased God to tender the hearts of some of them towards us; especially the Casseekey his wife, and some of the chiefest amongst them, who were made instruments to intercede for us, and stop the rage of the multitude, who seemed not to be satisfied without our blood. The Casseekey ordered some to swim, and fetch the canoe ashore; which being done, his wife came in a compassionate manner and took my wife out of the canoe, ordering her to follow her, which we did some distance from the inlet-side, and stood till all our people were brought over, which in a little time was done. But the rage of some was still great, thirsting to shed our blood, and a mighty strife there was amongst them: some would kill us, others would prevent it. And thus one Indian was striving with another. All being got over, [we] were to walk along the seashore to their town: in this passage we most of us felt the rage of some of them, either by striking or stoning, and divers arrows were shot: but those that were for preserving us would watch those that were for destroying us: and when some of them would go to shoot, others of them would catch hold of their bows or arm. It was so ordered that not one of us was touched with their arrows; several of us were knocked down, and some tumbled into the sea. We dared not help one another; but help we had by some of them being made instrumental to help us. My wife received several blows, and an Indian came and took hold of her hair, and was going either to cut her throat or something like it, having his knife nigh her throat; but I looked at him, making a sign that he should not, so he desisted: at which time another Indian came with a handful of sea-sand and filled our poor child's mouth. By this time the Casseekey's wife came to my wife seeing her oppressed, and they pulled the sand out of our child's mouth, and kept by my wife until we got into the Casseekey's house, which was about forty foot long and twenty-five foot wide, covered with palmetto leaves both top and sides. There was a range of cabins, or a barbecue on one side and two ends. At the entering on one side of the house a passage was made of benches on each side leading to the cabins. On these benches sat the chief Indians, and at the upper end of the cabin was the Casseekey seated. A kind of debate was held amongst them for an hour's time. After which Solomon and some others were called to the Casseekey; and were seated on the cabin; where the Casseekey talked to Solomon in the Spanish language, but could not hold a discourse. In a little time some raw deer skins were brought in and given to my wife and Negro women, and to us men such as the Indian men wear, being a piece of plat-work of straws wrought of divers colors and of a triangular figure, with a belt of four fingers broad of the same wrought together, which goeth about the waist and the angle of the other having a thing to it, coming between the legs, and strings to the end of the belt; all three meeting together are fastened behind with a horsetail, or a bunch of silk-grass exactly resembling it, of a flaxen color, this being all the apparel or covering that the men wear; and thus they clothed us. A place was appointed for us, mats being laid on the floor of the house, where we were ordered to lie down. But the place was extremely nasty; for all the stones of the berries which they eat and all the nastiness that's made amongst them lay on their floor, that the place swarmed with abundance of many sorts of creeping things; as a large black hairy spider, which hath two claws like a crab; scorpions; and a numberless number of small bugs. On these mats we lay, these vermin crawling over our naked bodies. To brush them off was like driving off mosquitoes from one where they are extreme thick. The Indians were seated as aforesaid, the Casseekey at the upper end of them, and the range of cabins was filled with men, women and children, beholding us. At length we heard a woman or two cry, according to their manner, and that very sorrowfully, one of which I took to be the Casseekey's wife which occasioned some of [us] to think that something extraordinary was to be done to us. We heard a strange sort of a noise which was not like unto a noise made by a man; but we could not understand what nor where it was; for sometimes it sounded to be in one part of the house, sometimes in another, to which we had an ear. And indeed our ears and eyes could perceive or hear nothing but what was strange and dismal; and death seemed [to have] surrounded us. But time discovered this noise unto us. The occasion of it was thus: In one part of this house where the fire was kept, was an Indian man, having a pot on the fire wherein he was making a drink of the leaves of a shrub (which we understood afterwards by the Spaniard, is called *casseena*), boiling the said leaves, after they had parched them in a pot; then with a gourd having a long neck and at the top of it a small hole which the top of one's finger could cover, and at the side of it a round hole of two inches diameter, they take the liquor out of the pot and put it into a deep round bowl, which being almost filled containeth nigh three gallons. With this gourd they brew the liquor and make it froth very much. It looketh of a deep brown color. In the brewing of this liquor was this noise made which we thought strange; for the pressing of this gourd gently down into the liquor, and the air which it contained being forced out of the little hole at top occasioned a sound; and according to the time and motion given would be various. This drink when made, and cooled to sup, was in a conch-shell first carried to the Casseekey, who threw part of it on the ground, and the rest he drank up, and then would make a loud He-m; and afterwards the cup passed to the rest of the Casseekey's associates, as aforesaid, but no other man, woman nor child must touch or taste of this sort of drink; of which they sat sipping, chatting and smoking tobacco, or some other herb instead thereof, for the most part of the day.

About noon was some fish brought us on small palmetto leaves, being boiled with scales, head and gills, and nothing taken from them but the guts; but our troubles and exercise were such that we cared not for food.

In the evening, we being laid on the place aforesaid the Indians made a drum of a skin, covering therewith the deep bowl in which they brewed their drink, beating thereon with a stick, and having a couple of rattles made of a small gourd put on a stick with small stones in it, shaking it, they began to set up a most hideous howling, very irksome to us, and some time after came some of their young women, some singing, some dancing. This was continued till midnight, after which they went to sleep.

The 8 month, 1; the 5 day of the week.
This day the Casseekey looking on us pleasantly, made presents to some of us, especially to my wife; he gave her a parcel of shellfish, which are known by the name of clams; one

or two he roasted and gave her, showing that she must serve the rest so, and eat them. The Indian women would take our child and suckle it, for its mother's milk was almost gone that it could not get a meal: and our child, which had been at death's door from the time of its birth until we were cast away, began now to be cheerful, and have an appetite to food. It had no covering but a small piece of raw deer skin; not a shred of linen or woollen to put on it.

About the tenth hour we observed the Indians to be on a sudden motion, most of the principal of them betook themselves to their houses: the Casseekey went to dressing his head and painting himself, and so also did the rest. When they had done, they came into the Casseekey's house, and seated themselves in order. In a small time after came an Indian with some small attendance into the house, making a ceremonious motion, and seated himself by the Casseekey, the persons that came with him seated themselves amongst the others. After some small pause the Casseekey began a discourse, which held nigh an hour. After which the strange Indian and his companions went forth to the waterside, unto their canoe lying in the sound, and returned presently with such presents as they had brought, delivering them unto the Casseekey, and those sitting by giving an applause. The presents were some few bunches of the herb they make their drink of, and another herb which they use instead of tobacco, and some platted balls stuffed with moss to lay their heads on instead of pillows. The ceremony being ended, they all seated themselves again, and went to drinking casseena, smoking and talking during the strangers' stay.

About noon some fish was brought us: hunger was grown strong upon [us], and the quantity given was not much more than each a mouthful; which we ate. The Casseekey ordered the master Joseph Kirle, Solomon Cresson, my wife and me, to sit upon their cabin to eat our fish; and they gave us some of their berries to eat. We tasted them, but not one amongst us could suffer them to stay in our mouths; for we could compare the taste of them to nothing else, but rotten cheese steeped in tobacco. Some time after we had eaten, some of the Indians asked us, if we were Spaniards. Solomon answered them, yes. Then some of the Indians would point to those whose hair was black, or of a deep brown, and say such a one was a Spaniard of the Havana, and such of Augustine: but those whose hair was of a light color they were doubtful of; some would say they were no Spaniards.

About the third hour in the afternoon the strangers went away, and some small time after they having satisfied themselves that most of us were Spaniards, told us that we should be sent for to the next town; and they told us that there was a *Nickaleer* off, and we understood them. "Englishmen off Bristol," also the number six men and a woman: and that they were to be put to death before we should get thither. We were silent, although much concerned to hear that report. They also told us that a messenger would come for us to direct us to the next town, thence to Augustine.

Night coming on they betook themselves to their accustomed singing and dancing. About the tenth or twelfth hour in the night before the singing and dancing was ended, came in a stranger armed with bow and arrows: the Casseekey and his companions entertained him with half an hour's discourse, which ended, we were on a sudden ordered to get up and hurried away with this stranger, they not giving us time to see if we were all together; and a troop of young Indian men and boys followed us for about four miles, all which way they pelted us with stones; at length they all left us except two and our guide; but we missed Solomon Cresson, and Joseph Kirle's boy, and Negro Ben; which was no small trouble to us.

We had not traveled above five miles before our guide caused to stop; and at some small distance was an Indian town, which I suppose our guide belonged to. Four Indians came thence with fire and water for him, and with palmetto leaves they made a blast of fire. Here we stayed nigh two hours: the flies were very thick and the night very cold, so that our naked bodies were not able to endure it but with grief. At length we left this place; the whole night following were troubled with these two young Indians, who at times would be abusing one or other of us, singling them out and asking if they were not *Nickaleer* or English? If they said, nay, then they would hit them a blow or more with a truncheon, which they had; and said, they were. We traveled all night without stopping from the aforesaid place.

8 month, 2; the 6 of the week.

After sun-rising we came up with the wreck of the vessel that we heard that was cast away. She was staved all to pieces, for her kelson was driven ashore. We saw sugar hogsheads, ginger and logwood; which gave us to suppose that it was one of our fleet, and we thought it to be either Burroughs or Smith, belonging to Bristol. A mile or more from hence we came to an inlet; our guide told us we must swim over, except my wife and Robert Barrow; but we signified that we could not. He carried Robert Barrow, Joseph Kirle, me, my wife and child over first; and at length the whole company, for it was a great way over. By that time we were all got over, the day was hot, and my wife quite tired [and] faint, as also Robert Barrow and Joseph Kirle, whose leg was grown so painful that it overcame him. We got under a grape bush for shelter from the sun. I sent one of my Negroes to seek for water for them; but there was none to be had; but he got some seaside-grapes, which with resting refreshed the weak and lame.

Our guide was for forcing us forward; so we traveled about four or five miles further, and met with the Casseekey of this town and commander of the northern part of this coast. He was an ancient man, his beard and hair gray. He inquired for the captain, so our people pointed to Joseph Kirle whom he went to and embraced him; then he asked for our mate or pilot. This man could speak Spanish better than any we had met with yet; but not so well as to discourse, only to ask some questions, and we had three or four amongst us could make a shift to answer him, for Solomon was kept behind. This old Casseekey seemed to have compassion on us, and said that those people who had served us thus in stripping of us were rogues. But we were his *comerradoes*, or friends, withal he said in [some] few days, he would carry us to Augustine; and thereupon he told us of six Englishmen, and one woman, being at his town. We inquired if he intended them for Augustine. But he would shake his head and point to the southward, saying, *Nickaleer*, no *comerradoe* (Englishmen were not his friends), which words were unpleasant to us. This people kept us company till we came within a mile or two of their town, and then they left us, they going faster got in before us. Their town stood about half a mile from the seashore within the land on the sound, being surrounded with a swamp, in which grew white mangrove trees, which hid the town from the sea. We were directed to the Casseekey's house, which was large, and filled with Indians, and then ordered to sit down. The Old Casseekey fetched some water, and washed Robert Barrow's feet, and my wife's; after which he got some canvas and crocus ginger bags, which they had got out of the vessel that was cast on shore; which was distributed amongst us. Joseph Kirle had a coat given him, which they had taken from the people of the other vessel; but it was rent down the back. My wife had two pieces of sail-canvas given her; and I with others had each a crocus ginger bag. They gave a piece of a barber's old linen shirt in bigness of a small handkerchief to cover our child. This was all our clothing. Robert Barrow and my wife were quite spent with traveling barefoot on the hot sand, having bruised their feet, and with stumps, stones and prickles, their feet, especially Robert Barrow's had holes in them, that one might have put the top of one's thumb in. We were directed to lie down on a cabin. The other vessel's company were one John Smith, master of the *Nantwitch*, a bark belonging to Bristol, which came out of Jamaica with us, with five men and one woman, viz. Andrew Murray, merchant, Andrew Barnes, mate, Hugh Allen, John Osler, John Shears and Cornelius Toker; two boys with a woman passenger named Penelope. We took an opportunity to discourse them. They were cast away the same night we were, and their vessel being forced by the storm (they not being able for two days before to carry any sail) on shore, they got into their boat and so on shore. And in a small time was a great part of their wreck driven on shore; amongst which, was a barrel or more of water, some barrels of beef or pork, with their chests, and many other things which they got. On the morrow they designed to travel to the northward. But Andrew Barnes their mate having been a long time afflicted with a flux which had wasted his body to skin and bone, so that he was not able to help himself, they left him and traveled a mile or more and came to the inlet which they could not pass. Whereupon they returned back again to take their boat; but at their return, before they could get away with their boat, they espied the Indians coming on them, who soon got to them; asked in Spanish what nation they were. If Spaniards, English, or French. But the Indians made signs to give them their clothing; which they readily did. But still they inquired of what nation. At first they answered, Spaniards; but the natives looked so furiously that they soon answered them, Englishmen. Thereupon every one had it, *Nickaleer, Nickaleer*. And then they very eagerly stripped them of all that they had on them: after which they drove them away to the northward unto their town; but Andrew Barnes not being able to stand nor go, was left behind, after they had stripped him, on the land naked when they were driven away. Before they got to the town, the Indian Casseekey gave them some clothing, and no violence was offered to their persons. They had plenty of fish and berries to the time of our coming. John Smith and Andrew Murray had their being in the Casseekey's house, and the woman named Penelope. The rest of Smith's people lodged in other Indian houses. But on our coming, the Old Casseekey told them, they must turn out, and make room for the Spaniards: but Smith and Murray would not go; and the Indian did not force them out. In some time after we had been in the house, came in Indian women laden with baskets of berries, mostly of the palm, some seaside coco-plums and seaside grapes: of the two latter we could eat; but of the palm-berries we could not bear the taste in our mouths. We laid ourselves on the cabin, on that part which was appointed us; on the other part the Young Casseekey or king lay being parted by a chest that stood thereon. Before night was a parcel of large fish called drums brought in: the Old Casseekey told Joseph Kirle, that those were for the Spaniards, and bid him let somebody to dress them. He also ordered us a pot. They were soon dressed, and we eat them. Night being come the Old Casseekey inquired about our losses; which we, as well as we could, gave him to understand that in our vessel was a great deal of clothing and money, which the Indians at Hoé-Bay had taken from us. He understood so much of the matter that he grew covetous, and said, he would go and get some of it from them.

About midnight came Solomon Cresson in a canoe with two Indians. The Old Casseekey began to examine him concerning our vessel, goods and money, or plate; which Solomon rendered a further account unto him of than we could; which caused him to resolve, on the morrow to provide men and boats, and to go down the sound to Hoebay, to have part from them; he would have had Solomon to have gone with him, but Solomon refused.

We inquired of Solomon concerning his stay and of the Negro Ben, and Joseph Kirle's boy. He said that he was stayed by force; but the Negro and the boy were asleep in another house when we were driven away. They had a design in staying of Solomon which he could not rightly understand; but supposed that they doubted that we were not all Spaniards; for the Indians of St. Lucie would say Solomon that he was a Spaniard, and some others; but the most of us were not Spaniards; and that they had stolen Solomon: but Solomon denied it.

The 8 month, 3; the 7 day of the week.
This morning the Old Casseekey with two canoes and ten Indians with him went hence for Hoe-Bay. He promised us that as soon as he returned, he would carry us to Augustine:

which he supposed would be in six days, if he had good weather. But this day the wind was got to the northeast, and it looked as though the weather would be stormy. The wind increased, and towards evening the water in the sound did rise that it began to cover the land, and came into the houses; but we had little or no rain till night: then the wind increased and rain also.

The 8 month, 4; the 1 day of the week.

This morning the wind was violent with rain; the king's house was knee-deep with water, and like to continue rising. I removed with my wife, child, Robert Barrow and Benjamin Allen to an Indian house that stood on a hill of oyster shells. In this house we remained this day; the wind continuing at northeast very violent, and by reason of much rain, the water rising every hour, the Indians began to put their dry berries into their canoes, and to seek which way to secure them. Several Indians betook themselves to their boats and carried what they had to some high land a considerable distance, where a place was made for their Casseekey or king. But before day, the house we were in was afloat, and the Indians were for turning us out, bidding us take an old canoe that had a hole in the side of her almost at the bottom big enough for a man to put his hand through; so that she was full of water: in this canoe they would have had us shift for ourselves; but we were not willing to go: the Indians made signs for us to be gone divers times. At length they grew angry, and took my kinsman Allen into the canoe, and carried him away: in a little time after returned with the canoe and bid me and Robert Barrow be gone. By this time day appeared, the wind and rain still violent. I then saw a house on another oyster hill that the water was not got over yet; to which I got and asked by signs if I might be there. The Indians seemed willing: so thither I got my wife, child, and Robert Barrow, and remained there. All this day the wind was violent, it rained and the flood continued. We imagined that the sea was broke in upon the land, and that we should be drowned. The house was almost blown to pieces, and the Indians often a-tying and mending it. The chief man of this house caused his wife to suckle our child; for it was almost famished, its mother having no milk in her breast; for we had received no sustenance since the storm began: fresh water was not to be had, the land being covered with the sea. The Indians offered us some of their berries, which we endeavored to eat; but could not; the taste was so irksome and ready to take our breath from us, when we tried to eat them; but we expected that if the flood continued longer, we should not need for water. Yet nevertheless we enjoying health and strength, and hunger growing violent, we would be tasting the berries, though we would reap no satisfaction.

The 8 month, 6; the 7 of the week.

This morning the flood began to come into this house also; the Indians seemed much concerned: the storm of wind and rain held till about mid-day; at which time the wind shifted southwest, with the rain; but in some few hours the flood began to abate.

The 8 month, 7; the 4 of the week.

By this day noon the water fell many feet, and I went out to see our people whom I left in the king's house: I found them where I left them. All the Indians had left the house; and our people remained on the cabin, which was about four foot from the floor. The flood had risen within two or three inches of the top of the cabin, and they said, they expected to die there. We began to express our hunger and thirst each to other: but there was no help as yet for either. We went to the springs, but they were all salt as the sea, and we would be striving with the berries; but they were so offensive unto us that we could reap no satisfaction from them. We went a-begging at times to the Indian women to suckle our child; which they would seldom deny.

The 8 month, 8; the 5 of the week.

This day we got some water to drink; but it was very brackish, and at best not very good.

The 8 month; 9; the 6 of the week.

This day the Young Casseekey returned to his house with his chests and other things.

The 8 month, 10; the 7 of the week.

This day we got a meal of fish the greatest plenty we had received since we were here. We longed for the Old Casseekey's return, and feared that this bad weather would lengthen the time.

The 8 month, 11; the 1 of the week.

This morning early came a messenger giving an account that the Old Casseekey was within some few leagues of the town, and that we might expect him this forenoon; within the time he came in sight. We all drew down to the water-side to receive him; we perceived he came in state, having his two canoes lashed together with poles athwart from the one to the other, making a platform, which, being covered with a mat, on it stood a chest, which was belonging to us, and my Negro boy Caesar, which the Casseekey of Hoe-Bay took from me, whom he had got from the Indians at Hoe-Bay. Upon this chest he sat cross-legged, being newly painted red, his men with poles setting the canoes along unto the shore. Seeing us, he cried "Wough" and looked very sternly at us. He was received by his people with great homage, holding out his hands (as their custom is) to be kissed, having his chest carried before him unto his house, whither he went, the house being filled with Indians. The Old Casseekey began and held a discourse for some hours, giving an account, as we suppose, what he heard and saw; in which discourse he would often mention *Nickaleer;* which caused us to fear that all things were not well. After he had told his story, and some of the elder Indians had expressed their sentiments thereof, they drank casseena and smoked until evening. The house being clean, the Old Casseekey looking very unpleasantly, showed unto us several things which he had got; as a hatchet, a knife, the chest and many other things, asking us, if they were not ours. Which we owned; whereupon he would say, they were *Nickaleer* (or

English). We signified that we had them of the English, but our money was Spanish. Towards the evening Joseph Kirle, myself and Solomon got an opportunity to discourse him; we began to urge his promise of carrying us for Augustine. At first he stated his hardships and labor to Hoe-Bay and back, and that he must have time to rest, before he could go out again; then he told us the way was long and would be tedious, and that at several places we must draw the canoes over land for a great distance; he also mentioned how many towns there were between this and Augustine, in number ten; but nigh the conclusion, he setting an angry countenance upon us, told us that at Hoe-Bay he was informed that we should say, we were all Englishmen; after he said this, in an angry manner he turned from us and went away.

This laid all our hopes in the dust, and we soon perceived the Indians grew jealous of us; for they would now daily be asking us, if we were not *Nickaleer?* or English? And would not seem satisfied with a denial. Many days were spent, and the time drew nigh that we understood the Old Casseekey was intended for Augustine; hereupon we applied ourselves to him, requesting that if all might not go, he would carry some of us; but he told us, he would carry but one. This put us on querying which of us should be that one. The generality was for me: but I and Joseph Kirle were for Solomon, because he could speak the Spanish language well, and no other of us could: and should any other of us have gone and come amongst those Indians to the northward, who we supposed could speak the Spanish language well, we should be discovered to be what these people did suppose we were; therefore it might overthrow all our expectations; but Solomon might pass all those objections. These reasons did not satisfy our people so that some of them grew choleric: of which the Old Casseekey took notice, and told Solomon, that if they made such a stir, he would not carry one. If he did, it should be either Solomon, Joseph Kirle, or me: whereupon we prevailed with him that Solomon might go, and accordingly made preparations, the Casseekey appointing the number of

Indians to go with him; also a canoe was sent for, which when it came, we found it to have belonged to the English, by the maker of her. This canoe had a great hole in the head nigh the bottom with many very great rents and holes in her: Joseph Kirle and I were required to mend her which with much ado was accomplished, the canoe being much decayed and rotten where the rents were.

The 8 month, 18; the 1 day of the week.

This day morning the Old Casseekey with Solomon and six Indians in a canoe set out for Augustine. The Casseekey carried a small chest, in which was nigh one hundred pieces-of-eight, as some of our people did suppose, with some other matters that were gotten from our vessel. The weather was likely for rain, which caused us to fear, should the weather prove bad, that Solomon would hardly live to get to Augustine; for he had nothing to cover him, except a pair of Indian breeches and a small piece of skin that covered his breast.

We understood by the Old Casseekey that it would be a month or next new-moon before we could expect their return; all which time we spent in much trouble and hardship. The weather began to grow cold, and provisions very short, that is palm berries, coco plums and sea-grapes, (which are the three sorts before expressed) the time of these fruits' bearing being over, they having no sort of fruit till next spring.

These people neither sow nor plant any manner of thing whatsoever, nor care for anything but what the barren sand produce; fish they have as plenty as they please but sometimes they would make it scarce to us, so that a meal in a week was most commonly our portion, and three meals a rarity. After the Old Casseekey's departure our hardships increased, especially my wife's and child's; for want of food of any sort, my wife's milk was gone, and our poor child was in great want; the Indians now and then would give it suck, but rarely to satisfy it; for there was a woman or two of their own which had young children and no breast to suckle them. Our extremity was such that any manner of thing would go down with us; the gills and guts of fish, picked off a dung-hill, was acceptable; the scraps the Indians threw away and the water they boiled their fish in, we were thankful for, though never so undecently handled by them. And though my wife had hardly any milk for our child, yet an Indian woman who was lately delivered of a child, and had no milk in her breast, would have her to suckle her child: which my wife consented unto. And this was a means of her and our child's reaping a benefit; for the Indians would give her fish, which means helped to increase milk for our child. Many were our exercises both in body and mind amongst this people. Sometimes they would look upon us as though they had some ill intent towards the whole of us: at other times they would tell us (who were nominally Spaniards) how and in what manner those of Smith's company should be put to death. And thus were we daily exercised in sorrow and grievous troubles. Sometimes doubts would arise amongst us concerning what would be the end of us, and what manner of death we should pass through. And whomsoever these doubts did appear in, it would be hard for another to help with counsel; but some there were whose hope never failed, they trusting in the Lord, to work for our deliverance. One thing did seem more grievous to me and my wife than any other thing. Which was that if it should so happen that we should be put to death, we feared that our child would be kept alive, and bred up as one of those people; when this thought did arise it wounded us deep.

This day being the time of the moon's entering the first quarter, the Indians have a ceremonious dance, which they begin about eight o'clock in the morning. In the first place comes an old man and takes a staff about eight foot long, having a broad arrow on the head thereof, and thence half way painted red and white like unto an barber's pole; in the middle of this staff is fixed a piece of wood shaped like unto thigh, leg and foot of a man, and the lower part thereof is painted black, and this staff being carried out of the Casseekey's house, is set fast in the ground standing upright. This done, he also brings out a basket containing six rattles, which are taken out

of the basket and placed at the foot of his staff; then another
old man comes and sets up a howling like unto a mighty dog,
but beyond him for length of breath; withal making a procla-
mation. This being done, the most of them having painted
themselves, some red, some black, some with black and red;
with their belly girt up as tight as well they can girt themselves with ropes, having their sheaves of arrows at their backs
and their bows in their hands, being gathered together about
this staff; six of the chiefest men in esteem amongst them,
especially one who is their doctor, and much esteemed, taking
up the rattles begins a hideous noise, standing round this staff,
taking their rattles, and bowing, without ceasing, unto the
staff for about half an hour; whilst these six are thus employed, all the rest are staring and scratching, pointing upwards and downwards on this and the other side every way;
looking like men frighted, or more like Furies: thus behaving
themselves until the six have done shaking their rattles. Then
they all begin a dance, violently stamping on the ground for
the space of an hour or more without ceasing. In which time
they will sweat in a most excessive manner, that by the time
the dance is over, what by their sweat and the violent stamping of their feet, the ground is trodden into furrows; and by
the morning, the place where they danced was covered with
maggots. Thus often repeating the manner they continue till
about three or four o'clock in the afternoon; by which time
many were sick and fainty. And then being gathered into the
Casseekey's house, they sit down, having some hot casseena
ready, which they drink plentifully; and give greater quanti-
ties thereof to the sick and fainty than to others; then they eat
berries. On these days they eat not any food till night.

The next day about the same time, they begin their dance as
the day before. Also the third day they begin their dance at
the usual time: at which time came many Indians from other
towns, and fell to dancing without taking any notice one of
the other.

This day they were stricter than the other two days, for no

woman must look upon them; but if any of their women go out of their houses, they go veiled with a mat.

The 8 month, 28;* the 1 of the week.

This day was a day of plenty unto us, for we had as much fish and berries as would serve us two days.

This week we observed that great baskets of dried berries were brought in from divers towns and delivered to the king or Young Casseekey, which we supposed to be a tribute to the king of this town, who is chief of all the towns from St. Lucie to the northward of this town of Jece.

The 27; the 3 of the week.

This day was a bag of berries (the bag made of grass) given us, which we eat in two or three days; and then we fasted as many days before the Young Casseekey would give us more.

About this time John Smith and Andrew Murray were sharply seized with a fever and ague: when the fit of the ague was on them, the Indians would mock and deride them. This we well observed, that these people had no compassion on their own aged declining people when they were past their labor, nor on others of their own which lay under any declining condition: for the younger is served before the elder, and the elder people both men and women are slaves to the younger.

In this place we saw many tokens of some of our nation's having fallen into the hands of these people. As two English canoes, one of cedar the other of cotton tree like those of Jamaica, several blocks and sheaves of lignum-vitae; several tools and knives, and more particularly, a razor, on the haft of which was writ the man's name, thus, THOMAS FOS-TER. Some of these things looked as though they had been several years amongst them, some but a few. But we never dared to inquire; for we thought they brought some things in our view to try us.

Here was a man in this town who, some years past, had

---

* "25" in MS. copy.

been taken off by some of our English sloops, for a diver on the wreck to the eastward of Cuba, where he was sometime: but the vessel putting into Cuba, for water, this Indian swam on shore and got to the Havana, thence to St. Augustine, and so to his native town. The greatest charge this man had against the English was for taking him and their people away; not but that he was well used amongst them. This Indian would often call Joseph Kirle, Solomon Cresson and some of us into his house, seeming very cheerful, asking if they would eat, withal asking the name of the berries, expecting we would call them after the English manner "Plums" but perceiving his drift, and having learned the name of them, as the Spaniard calls them "Vivaes"; then he would tell us that the English called them "Plums": such sort of discourse we had at times, for he would be striving to trap us, viz. Joseph, Solomon and me, in words; but he never had an advantage, for when Solomon was gone, we shunned all his invitations and arguments.

The 8 month, 31; the 7 of the week.

This day came in a canoe laden with fish, and it was free, for those that would, to take as much as they pleased. The Indians put us to go and take; for it was a kind of a scramble amongst us and the young Indian men and boys. All of us got fish enough to serve us two or three days.

The 9 month, 2; the 2 of the week.

This morning about sun-rising came two strange Indians, who had run so hard that they sweated extremely, of whom we understood that the Spaniards were coming with their Old Casseekey; which news surprised us, doubting the truth of it, for Solomon had been gone but sixteen days, and we understood that they must have an extraordinary passage to be here in a month. We had not long to consider of the matter, for in an hour's time we heard four muskets discharged, and immediately we looked out, and the Spaniards in their piragua were in sight. The Indians were like a people amazed and overcome with fear: we perceived the noise of a gun was terrible unto them. The Spaniards landed being in number twelve, one Sebastian Lopez commanding ten soldiers, with one Indian an interpreter. The Spaniards embraced us very cheerfully, and expressed their being glad to find us alive. But we were not able to discourse each other, though we had so much Spanish as to ask questions, and answer some part of what they asked us. One of the Spaniards said they could not speak English, nor could we speak Spanish enough to understand each other sufficiently: this the Indians perceived and immediately cried out, *Nickaleer, Nickaleer*, and looked enviously on us, so that, could they have had their wills, we believed they would not have suffered us to have lived many hours; but the Spaniards awed them.

We received a letter from Solomon which he writ when he met with Captain Sebastian Lopez, signifying the government of Augustine's great care for our preservation, of what nation soever we were. But how these persons, or the governor of Augustine had knowledge of us, we could not understand; for they had been fourteen days from Augustine, which was nigh the time Solomon went hence, and they met Solomon about half way, and sent him for Augustine with other guides, bringing the Old Casseekey and his people with them. We observed that the Old Casseekey seemed much dejected. We supposed the Spaniards had taken from him the money and what other things he had carried with him; or that he was vexed he should be so deceived in taking us for Spaniards.

The Spaniards were extraordinary kind unto us, so that we had occasion to rejoice, and thank the Lord for this part of our deliverance by this means. They were also a terror unto the Indians; for they searched their houses and took all from them that ever they could find, even to the stub of a nail: which aggravated them, and increased their disaffection to us-ward; so that we dared not to stir from a Spaniard. The Spanish captain made inquiry where we were cast away, and what was saved that we had in our vessel? We gave an account so well as we could to make him understand us: which

account made him very desirous to go down thither; but looking over a paper often, which we supposed, was the governor's
order and instructions to him, we understood they would not
permit him to prosecute that design: beside we made him
sensible of the danger we should be in, if he and his men
should go and leave us amongst these people who were so
bitterly incensed against us.

They inquired what became of the boat that belonged to
Smith's vessel and ours. We told them that these Indians had
taken Smith's boat and sunk her somewhere in the sound; but
ours was at St. Lucie. The Spaniards made the Indians go and
show where they had sunk Smith's boat and help our people
to get her up: which being done, she was brought to the town:
the Spaniards were mightily pleased with her, and proposed
that they in their canoe, and our people in that boat should go
to Hoe-Bay, whereby they might get all from the Indians
which they had gotten from us. But we would not countenance the matter; we were for a speedy departing from
amongst these people as we could, since it had pleased God to
open a way for our deliverance.

This morning the Spanish captain made the Indians provide two canoes, which he caused to be lashed together at some
distance with sticks across, and matted on the top: which
being done, with four Indians, Joseph Kirle, John Smith,
Robert Barrow, Andrew Murray, Benjamin Allen, Nathaniel
Randall, John Shears, Cornelius Toker, Joseph Kirle's boy
John Hilliar; four Negroes, viz. Jack, Caesar, Sarah, and
Quenza were sent away for Augustine: but not one morsel of
victuals, except a very few berries, had they with them; and
not one Spaniard to guard them, but were put under the government of those four Indians. About an hour after Joseph
Kirle was gone the Spanish captain ordered Smith's boat to be
made ready with two Spaniards, and four of our men to row
to the place where the drift of Smith's vessel was, to look for
log-wood or old iron: when they returned, there was not anything of value.

But our people said as they were searching about they

found the bones of Andrew Barnes: his skull and jaw-bone were broken; which occasioned us to suspect that he was knocked on the head by the Indians, after they had driven away Smith and his people.

We told the Spanish captain that Joseph Kirle's Negro Ben had been absent ever since the day after Solomon Cresson went hence, being gone with the Old Casseekey's wife, but we knew not whither. The captain made inquiry of the Indians whither he was gone. They said, for Hoe-Bay; then he ordered them to send for him, for he would not leave him behind. The Indians said he would be here within a day or two. The Spaniards were continually searching for what they could find of such things as the Indians had gotten from us or others: and when they could find no more, they would offer to buy with tobacco, what they could persuade the Indians to bring to light. A leaf or half of leaf of tobacco would purchase a yard of linen or woollen, or silk from the Indians. Such admirers of tobacco are they, that they esteem it beyond any other thing. An Indian of the town some time before the Spaniards came, having a considerable quantity of ambergris boasted that when he went for Augustine with that, he could purchase of the Spaniards a looking-glass, an ax, a knife or two, and three or four *mannocoes* (which is about five or six pounds) of tobacco. The quantity of ambergris might be about five pound weight.

The 9 month, the 4; the 4 of the week.
This day we made oars for Smith's boat of sticks and the cantle-pieces of sugar hogsheads which were gotten on the beach when the drift of Smith's vessel came on shore. And this evening came the Old Casseekey's wife with Joseph Kirle's Negro Ben and Joseph Kirle's boat; which was of great advantage to help to carry us. We worked all this night to fit the boat and oars unto her, being intended to go away as soon as we could complete that job.

The Spaniards had brought little provision with them, so that there was not much to spare for us; having not above a rove of corn, and a little Nova Spain bread, which was so bad that it was more dust and dead weevils than bread: an handful of it was an acceptable present to us. We would mix it with a little water, making it to a paste, which would eat pleasantly; but hunger was no stranger unto us; and we knew not that we should have any victuals on our journey: but our deliverance seemed to overbalance all. The Indians would not give us any berries: but our people watched an opportunity and took one of the Casseekey's bags of berries, which might contain about a bushel; which was all that one-and-thirty of us had to depend upon.

The 9 month, 5; the 5 of the week.

This morning about three hours before day we departed from this town of Jece; the weather was grown cold; we had nothing wherewith to cover our bodies, besides what the Indians gave us at first, except my wife, for whom the Spaniards got an old jacket (which had been one of Smith's men's), and gave her to wear; also a small piece of cloth to cover our poor child; but it pleased God to strengthen us in this our condition, so that we rowed all this day without ceasing until three hours after it was dark, by which time we got to an Indian town. Here we met with Joseph Kirle, Robert Barrow, and the others, who got thither not above an hour or two before us. They had not received any manner of sustenance from the time they left us, until they got some berries of us, having lain one night of the two in a swamp: but they were as cheerful as men could be in this strait.

Since they left us, amongst their other hardships, Joseph Kirle had like to have lost his life several times. The first was thus. Whilst the two canoes were lashed together, having a few berries that were designed to have been shared amongst them; the Irish boy Cornelius Toker would ever and anon be taking some of them, who being often reproved by Joseph Kirle and others; would not desist; whereupon Joseph Kirle with the paddle he paddled the canoe along with struck him; thereupon an Indian took his bow and arrow and was going to shoot Joseph, who seemed little concerned whether he lived or died, withal saying the Spaniards would justify him.

Another time when he was spent with paddling the canoe, and desired John Smith, Andrew Murray, and others of them as well able as himself to give him a spell, which they refused, and he being not able to paddle further, laid down his paddle; whereupon the Indians commanding him to paddle, he refused, saying, they might kill him if they would, opening his breast for them to execute their wills; which they seemed as though they would have done: but after great threatening they desisted.

Another time the wind being high and the seas rough that they were forced to unlash their canoes, by Joseph Kirle's persuasion, and to go single; Joseph Kirle taking one canoe to his own management, having Robert Barrow, his boy, my kinsman, Nathaniel Randall, and the Negroes in her; which being thus single from the other company was more satisfactory to him than before, though none to help but Nathaniel Randall. My Negro woman named Sarah, having beaten and abused a girl named Quenza, being reproved often by him and Robert Barrow, she therefore abused them in an extraordinary manner; whereupon Joseph struck her with his paddle; at which one of the Indians in the other canoe took his striking staff and darted at him, narrowly missing him.

[*9 mo: 6: 6*] This morning Joseph Kirle with those that were with him were by the Spanish captain ordered away at break of day; he not taking any care to give them a little sustenance; and about an hour or two after we followed, rowing all this day without ceasing until an hour or two in the night: by which time we got to an Indian town, where not any thing was to be had but water. About two hours after us came Joseph Kirle.

The Spanish captain would not let them come on shore, but ordered them to keep on, that we might get next night to the place where we must haul our boats over land, from one sound unto another.

The 9 month, 7; the 7 of the week.
This morning we set forward very early and rowed hard:

about noon we got to a parcel of marshy islands, amongst which we were to go up creeks. The passage was very difficult to find. At length when we were got nigh an Indian town, the Spaniards hallooed, and an Indian came out into the marsh, but was very loath to come near us. At length he came wading to us to be our pilot. We set forward, and in an hour's time or more were got to the place where Joseph Kirle and those with him were; the Indians that were with Joseph would not let them proceed further until we came up with them. In half an hour's time we got to the place where we were to haul our boats over land, being about a quarter of a mile from sound to sound: at this place the sea was half a furlong from us. The Spanish captain gave the Indian we last took in a piece of a leaf of tobacco commanding him to go with all speed and bid his Casseekey with all his able men come to help to haul our boats over land. But we set to work, and had them over by that time the Indians came. The Spanish captain gave the Casseekey a leaf or two of tobacco for him and discharged them, only ordered the Casseekey to send some men a-fishing for him, which they did, and within night brought a stately parcel of fish; but none of our people had any part of it except my wife, and Penelope. What they did not eat they kept to carry with them.

A little before night sprang up a storm of wind at northeast. It seemed likely to be a dismal night of wind and rain, and we were got to a place where there was not a tree, or bush, or any manner of shelter, and the wind so very cold that we thought that we should not live till the next day. We had no wood to make a fire with, and what to do we could not tell, but we were resolved to try to get some, and in order thereto, some of the ablest of us went along the bay to search for driftwood, and found a little, but rain came with the night and no shelter to be had but our boats; and the Spaniard would not let us meddle with them to turn them bottom upwards for shelter: which seemed very hard, but they made themselves some shelter with mats. We were forced to exercise patience, and with what salt-water wood we had, made as good a fire

In 1934 Dr. Andrews with his wife Evangeline, leased the old DuBois home on the ancient shell mound south of *Jupiter Inlet.* — DuBois Home 1975 — *Photo by Patricia Albee.*

They learned that the pre-historic shell mound upon which they lived was the site of the *Village of Hobe* where the Dickinson party was held captive. Shell mound about 1900 — *Photo: courtesy John and Bessie DuBois.*

"I would push my skiff far up the twisting mangrove creeks that led in from *Peck's Lake* to the sea beach at the center of *Jupiter Island*." — *Photo by Patricia Albee*

"How amazing it was to come out from the dark tunnels of the mangrove creeks bordered by the twisted trees on their spidery roots into the bright white light of the sea beach, streaching out of sight in both directions — utterly devoid of people." — *Photo by John C. Hutchins*

"There was the eternal rustle of shells being chewed by the surf, sand fleas digging down frantically in the receding surges." — *Photo by Patricia Albee*

"we supposed the sound was a great river; and therefore were not willing to take his advice, having no knowledge; but his councel was good, as we found afterwards; for the conveniency of passage." — *Photo by Patricia Albee*

"This morning we get forward very early and rowed hard: about noon we got to a parcel of marshy islands. Amongst which we were to go up creeks." — *Photo by John Whiticar*

"A little before night sprang up a storm of wind at northeast. It seemed likely to be a dismal night of wind and rain, and we were got to a place where there was not a tree, or bush, or any matter of shelter, and the wind so very cold that we thought that we should not live till the next day." — *Photo by Patricia Albee*

"Our Indian guide said, we might get to a town about two leagues off; which we were glad to hear, for it rained hard so we with our guide set foreward and walked over a parcel of scraggy shrubby hills to the seashore, along which we traveled till we got to the Indian town, where we got plenty of berries for our supper. — *Photo by John C. Hutchins*

"We departed and met with intricate passage; for sometimes we should be aground on oyster banks or shoals, and almost out of sight of land." — *Photo by John Whiticar*

"Poor Robert Barrow was a great way behind us: I feared we should never see him again." — *Photo by Joseph Noble*

"This morning we put on shore having passed an inlet of the sea and here we dressed some victuals and got a little sleep until the tide served." — *Photo by Patricia Albee*

Jupiter Island Beach, site of the wreck of the "Reformation" —*Photo by Patricia Albee.*

as we could, and laid ourselves down on the sand by it: and it pleased God we had a comfortable night beyond our expectation: only the cold was very sharp.

The 9 month, 8; the 1 of the week.

This morning we set forward; but the water was so low that we were forced to wade and thrust the boat along for some miles. At length we got into a deep channel, where was nothing to be seen but marsh and water, and no fast land, nor trees.

About ten o'clock we heard three or four muskets fired a little ahead of us in the channel we were in. Our Spaniards presently answered them with the like, and in a little time we met. This was a piragua to join with that came for us, having order to go to the place where we were cast away, and to get what was to be had from the Indians: but this other boat turned back, for there was no place to go on shore; and in an hour or two's time we got into the other sound where the land was not to be seen from side to side in some places. The like was in the other we came through. About an hour before sunset we got to an Indian plantation (this was the first place we saw anything planted) being full of pumpion vines and some small pumpions on them but the Spaniards were too quick for us and got all before us: some of us got a few as big as one's fist. We had a fire there, yet had not patience to dress them as they should be, but put them into the fire, roasted them and eat them. The Spaniards used a great deal of cookery with their pumpions, and the piragua that came last from Augustine had brought bread, corn and strung beef; but it was kept from us, except a piece of strung beef the captain of the Spaniards gave my wife as big as a stick of sealing-wax; which we treasured up, expecting it must be harder with us when we left these people. Here Captain Sebastian Lopez drew up a writing, and would have had me and Joseph Kirle to sign it; which we refused: for we perceived he had a design especially against me, to oblige me to give him some of my Negroes. We answered him short; that I reckoned myself and Negroes at the Governor of Augustine's disposal; and we would sign no writing. We borrowed a pot and boiled pumpion leaves, having nothing to put to them but water, which was satisfactory; but this night was more terrible than the last, the wind being at northwest; it did not blow hard, yet it was very cold, we lieing in an open field without any shelter; one side of us would scorch while the other was freezing. Our Negro woman Hagar's little boy named Cajoe was seized with convulsion fits about two in the morning which was chiefly occasioned by the cold and want of food: but help there was not from us. The Spanish captain came to see the child, and supposing that it would die, asked if the child was a Christian? He was answered, as good a one as he could make it; but he called for some water, putting some of it on the crown of the child's head, and crossing it, called him Francisco. This action pacified its father and mother.

The 9 month, 9; the 2 of the week.

This morning we were to go forward and the Spaniards were to return to the place where we were cast away: but our two boats would not carry us all; therefore we had the Spaniards great piragua to carry us one day's journey further to an Indian town, and four Spaniards with us, three of which were to bring the piragua back, the other was to be our guide for Augustine. We departed and met with intricate passage; for sometimes we should be aground on oyster banks, or shoals, and almost out of sight of land. About two or three in the afternoon we had not water to go any further: the wind being northwesterly drove the water out of the sound: but being nigh the shore where had been an Indian town: we went on shore and found some ripe berries on the palm shrubs, which we were very earnest after till such time as a storm of wind with rain began to come upon us and night nigh at hand; whereupon we all got together, considering what we should do, since there was no possibility of getting shelter here. Our Indian guide said, we might get to a town about two leagues off; which we were glad to hear, for it rained hard so we with our guide set forward and walked over a parcel of scraggy shrubby hills to the seashore, along which we traveled till we got to the Indian town, where we got plenty of berries for our supper. It rained much till towards morning.

The 9 month. 10.

This morning the Indians were not willing to stay any longer; and we were by our guide required to depart; which we did, and a great many young Indian men followed us some miles along the bay, and offered violence to Robert Barrow and several others; but were easily stopped by showing them a rusty musket presented towards them, and so they left us. We had an untoward passage from the seashore athwart the land to the Indian town, the ground being swampy, and scraggy hills, which to our bare feet was very troublesome. This was a large town, and there was another large town about a mile distant in sight, thither part of our company was sent to be quartered: at which town about a twelvemonth since a parcel of Dutchmen were killed who, having been cast away on the Bohemia shoals, in a flat which they built escaped hither, and were here devoured by these cannibals, as we understood by the Spaniards. The flat or boat our people saw: but they seemed kind to them, giving them fish and berries to eat. We remained at these two towns till next morning. The Indians of the town I was at, were not so kind as those at the other town had been: some of our people were for selling their rags to the Indians for fish; but we thought 'twas most necessary, of the two extremes, to defend against the cold: for every day grew colder than other; and we feared that if we were much longer exposed to it, we should not live it out.

The 9 month, 11; the 4 of the week.

This morning leaving this town, we embarked in our two boats, and those of our people that were at the other town were to have a large canoe to carry them thence, and were to meet us in the sound. We rowed several leagues and did not meet them; it being then about ten o'clock; the Spaniard would go on shore and travel back by land to see after them. We being by an inlet of the sea which was a mile over, the

Spaniard ordered us to go on the other side, and there stay
for him; which we did many hours. At this place we all went
upon the search to see if anything was to be had for the belly,
some on the land, some in the water. The land yielded
nothing; but in the water we got a sort of shellfish called
Water-Soldiers, which we eat: at length the canoe with our
people came, but our Spaniard was not come; but in about
half an hour's time he came with a small canoe. This was the
place where Solomon met the Spaniards. The canoes had each
two Indians to set them along: and we had one Indian for our
guide named Wan-Antonia who the Spaniard said was a
Christian, but an inhabitant of that town where the Dutchmen were killed. We set forward in our two boats and the
two canoes, and rowed till night, being nigh a place of
thickety wood, which we made choice of to lodge at for this
night: here was wood enough. We made large fires, were
pleased with the place, and lay down to rest. About midnight
I had a great loss; having about a quart of berries whole, and
as much pounded to mix with water to feed our child with;
the fire being disturbed, the cloth which we had our food in
was burnt. All was lost, and nothing to be had until we could
get to the Spaniards, which was two days' march at least.
About an hour after this the wind rose at northwest, and it
began to rain; but having small palmetto which grew nigh,
Joseph Kirle and I set to work and made a shelter which
would keep ten or more of us from the weather. We had no
sooner completed our work, but it rained hard. In this shower
of rain the four Indians got from amongst us, took their
canoes, and away they went back again. When day appeared,
we missed them, upon which we went to the waterside, where
we found the two canoes gone. And now we were in a great
strait. But the Spaniard said those that could travel best must
go by land. The persons pitched upon were Richard Limpeney, Andrew Murray, Cornelius Toker, Joseph Kirle's boy,
John Hilliard, and Penelope with seven Negroes named
Peter, Jack, Caesar, Sarah, Bell, Susanna and Quenza. The
Spaniards and the Indian Wan-Antonia went with them to

direct them the way carrying them over land to the seashore, and then directing to keep the seashore along to the northward.

They returned to us, and we with our two boats rowed all day without ceasing till sunsetting: and when we put on shore, the place was an old Indian field on a high bleak hill where had been a large Indian house, but it was tumbled down. Of the ruins of this house we made a shelter against the northwest wind, which began to blow very bleak. The Spaniard went to the sea, which was not two miles off, to see if our people had passed, and at his return he said, they were gone by. We asked if they could reach to any house or Indian town for shelter? For we supposed, should they be without fire this night, they could not live. He said, they must travel all night. Night came on: We had fire and wood enough, and had gathered a great heap of grass to lie in, hoping to have got some rest. But the northwest increased, and the cold was so violent, that we were in a lamentable condition, not able to rest, for as we lay or stood so close to the fire that it would scorch us, that side from it was ready to freeze: we had no other way, but to stand and keep turning for the most part of the night. We all thought that we never felt the like. The Spaniard that was clothed was as bad to bear it as we that were naked. At length day appeared and we must go.

The 9 month, 13; the 6 of the week.

This morning, we were loath to part with our fires, but to stay here it could not be: so we went to our boats; wading in the water was ready to benumb us. But we put forward, and rowing about 2 leagues came to an old house, where the Spaniard told us we must leave the boats and travel by land; we had a boggy marsh to wade through for a mile to get to the seashore, and had about five or six leagues along the bay or strand to the Spanish sentinel's house. The northwest wind was violent, and the cold such that the strongest of us thought we should not out-live that day. Having got through the boggy marsh and on the seashore, our people, black and white, made all speed, one not staying for another that could not travel so fast; none but I with my wife and child, Robert Barrow, my kinsman Benjamin Allen and my Negro London, whom I kept to help carry my child, keeping together. The rest of our company had left us, expecting not to see some of us again; especially Robert Barrow, my wife and child. We traveled after as well as we could having gone about two miles the cold so seized on my kinsman Benjamin Allen that he began to be stiff in his limbs, and staggered and fell, grievously complaining that the cold would kill him. Our Negro having our young child I and my wife took our kinsman under each arm and helped him along; but at length his limbs were quite stiff, his speech almost gone, and he began to foam at [the] mouth. In this strait we knew not what to do; to stay with him we must perish also, and we were willing to strive as long as we could. We carried our kinsman and laid him under the bank, not being dead. I resolved to run after our people, some of them not being out of sight; which I did and left my wife and child with the Negro to follow as fast as they could. I run about two miles, making signs to them, thinking if they should look behind them and see me running, they would stop till I got up with them. I was in hopes that if I could have accomplished this my design, to have got help to have carried my kinsman along; but they stopped not, and I run until the wind pierced me so that my limbs failed and I fell; yet still I strove, and getting up walked backwards to meet my wife. As I was going I met with the Spaniard coming out of the sand-hills and Joseph Kirle's Negro Ben. I made my complaint to the Spaniard, but he not being able to understand me well, went forward. I then applied myself to the Negro, making large promises if he would fetch my kinsman; he offered to go back and use his endeavor, which he did. At length my wife and child came up with me; she was almost overcome with grief, expressing in what manner we were forced to part with our kinsman, and expecting that she and the child should go next.

Poor Robert Barrow was a great way behind us: I feared we should never see him again. I used my endeavor to comfort and cheer my wife, entreating her, not to let grief over-come her; I had hopes that the Lord would help us in this strait, as He hath done in many since we were in this land. And if it pleased God that we might lay down our lives in this wilderness, that we might beseech Him to enable us to do it willingly. Thus striving in a deep exercise of body and mind we traveled on, admiring God's goodness in preserving us thus far through so many eminent dangers. In the sense of which a secret hope would arise (though involved with human doubts and fear) that the Lord would yet preserve us. I took my child from the Negro and carried him. I had an Indian mat with a split in it, through which I put my head, hanging over my breast unto my waist: under this I carried my child, which helped to break the wind off it; but the poor babe was black with cold from head to foot, and its flesh as cold as a stone; yet it was not froward. Its mother would take it now and then and give it the breast, but little could it get at it; besides we dared not stop in the least, for if we did, we should perceive our limbs to fail. About two o'clock in the afternoon we came up with our Negro woman Hagar with her child at her back almost dead: and a little further we came up with our Negro girl Quenza, being dead, as we thought, for she was as stiff as a dead body could be, and her eyes set; but at length we per-ceived her breathe; but she had no sense, nor motion. We carried her from the waterside under the bank. This increased my wife's sorrow; and she began to doubt she should not be able to travel much further: but I endeavored to encourage her not to leave striving as long as any ability was left. All our people were out of sight except four, and those we had gained upon. I sent my Negro to overtake them, and to desire them to slacken their pace till we got up with them; being in hopes that gaining their company would [help] to cheer up my wife: but they would not; so the Negro stopped for us. We had lost sight of Robert Barrow by this time. Soon after we overtook John Smith who was one of the four: he began to fail, and his companions left him; whereupon he made griev-ous complaints which I reproved him for, lest he should discourage my wife. The sun was nigh setting; and we began to look out for the sentinel's post; and my Negro at times got upon several of the highest sand hills to look out, but could not see any house, nor the smoke of fire. This was terrible to us all, for the day being so cold, the night much more, and we not able to travel without rest, being a starved people both within our bodies and without, and if we ceased from traveling, we should instantly be numbed and move no further. In the midst of these reasonings and doubtings we were got into, I espied a man as I thought, standing on the bank but at great distance; I was afraid to speak lest it should prove otherwise, but he was soon seen by the whole company, and at length we espied him walking towards the land; this confirmed us, and so we took to the hills again to look out, yet could not see the house from thence, but on the next hill we saw it. This was joy unto us, though we began to have a sense of our tiredness, for our resolution abated after we had got sight of the house.

When we got to the house, we found four sentinels and the Spaniards our guide with three of our men; viz Joseph Buckley, Nathaniel Randall, and John Shears. The Spaniard bid us welcome, and made room for us to sit down by the fire. The chiefest man of the sentinel took a kersey coat and gave my wife to cover her, and gave each of us a piece of bread made of Indian corn, which was pleasant unto us: after it we had plenty of hot casseena drink. It was dark and we endeavored to prevail with the Spaniards to go seek for Robert Barrow and my kinsman, offering them considerable, but they seemed not fully to understand me, yet I could make them sensible that my kinsman was almost dead, if not quite; and that the old man was in a bad condition. They made me to understand that the weather was not fit to go out, but they would watch if Robert should pass by. About an hour or two after one of the Spaniards being walking out of the bay met with Robert and brought him into the house. We rejoiced to see him, and inquired concerning our kinsman and Negro Ben. He said our kinsman was striving to get up and could not; he came to him and spake unto him; he could not answer but cried, and he could not help him; but coming along at some considerable distance met Negro Ben; who said he was going for Benjamin Allen, so he passed him; and some miles further he saw Negro Jack drawing himself down from the bank, his lower parts being dead, and crying out for some fire that he might save his life; but he did not see the Negro girl whom we hauled out of the way. We were under a great concern for our kinsman; the Spaniards we could not prevail upon to go and fetch him, or go and carry wherewith to make a fire: which had they done and found them living, it might have preserved them. But we hoped Negro Ben would bring our kinsman. The Spaniards would have had most of us to have gone to the next sentinel's house; which was a league further; but we all begged hard of them to let us lie in their house in any place on the ground, for we were not able to travel further: besides the cold would kill us; for we were in such a trembling shaking condition, and so full of pain from head to foot, that it's not to be expressed. At length the Spaniards consented that Robert Barrow, I, my wife and child, and John Smith should lie in the house; but to Joseph Buckley, Nathaniel Randall, John Shears, and my Negro London, they would not grant that favor: so one of the Spaniards taking a fire-brand bid those four go with him. He directed them to a small thicket of trees and showed them to gather wood and make large fires and sleep there. These poor creatures lay out, and it proved a hard frosty night. The Spaniard returned and said they were got into a wood, and had fire enough. We were silent, but feared they would hardly live till morning.

After they were gone, the Spaniards took a pint of Indian corn and parched it and gave part to us, which we accepted cheerfully; also they gave us some casseena drink. We were in extraordinary pain, so that we could not rest; and our feet were extremely bruised, the skin was off and the sand caked with the blood that we could hardly set our feet to the ground after we had been some time in the house. The night was extreme cold though we were in the house; and by the fire we could not be warm, for one side did scorch whilst the other was ready to freeze: and thus we passed the night.

The 9 month, 14; the 7 of the week.

This morning we looked out, and there was a very hard frost on the ground, so it was terrible to go out of doors. Our people returned from the wood, but complained heavily of their hardship in the night. They had not been an hour in the house before the Spaniards gave us all a charge to be gone to the next sentinel's house: this was grievous to us all, but more especially to my wife, who could not raise herself when down; but go we must, for though we entreated hard for my wife and Robert Barrow, we could not prevail that they might stay until we could get a canoe. As we were all going one Spaniard made a sign for me and my wife to stay, which we did; and it was to have a handful of parched corn. As soon as we had received it they bid us be gone to the next sentinel's, where was victuals enough for us. The sun was a great height, but we could not feel any warmth it gave, the northwester beginning to blow as hard as it did the day before. And having deep sand to travel through, which made our traveling this one league very hard, especially to my wife and Robert. The Spaniards sent my wife a blanket to be left at the next sentinel's house.

At length we came to an inlet of the sea; on the other side was the look-out and sentinel's house: here were all our people sitting waiting to be carried over and in a little time came one of the sentinels, with a canoe and carried us over.

This sentinel would not suffer us to come into his house, but caused us to kindle a fire under the lee of his house and there sit down: about half an hour after he bid us be gone to the next sentinel's, which was a league further, giving us a cup of casseena and two quarts of Indian corn for us all, bidding us go to our company at next house and [get] our corn dressed there.

I understood that our Negro woman Hagar got hither late last night having her child dead at her back, which the Spaniards buried.

One of the Spaniards* went with us to the next inlet carrying a stick of fire to set fire of some trash to make a signal for them on the other side to fetch us over, the inlet being very wide. When the canoe came over for us, our guide took the blanket from my wife; but the Negro which brought over the canoe lent my wife one of his coats, so we got over, but before we got to the house we had a shower of hail. At this house we were kindly received, having such a mess of victuals as we had not had in a long time before, which was very pleasant to our hunger-starved stomachs. Our people went hence, this morning, for Augustine, having a guide with them: but John Hosler and Penelope were left here, not being able to travel. We remained here till the morrow, but the night was so extreme cold that we could not rest.

The 9 month, 15; the 1 of the week.
This morning the Spaniards bid us prepare to travel for they were not able to maintain us. We understood that it was five or six leagues to Augustine, and we could not travel so far, being all of us lamed and stiff: we entreated them to let us go in a canoe, but they denied us: we entreated for the two women and Robert Barrow; at length we prevailed that they should go up in a canoe, for the canoe was to go whether we went or not.

While all this discourse was, came in a couple of Spaniards, one being the sentinel that went with our people the day before, the other was a person the governor had sent with a canoe and four Spaniards to fetch us. This was cheerful news; for had we gone to have traveled without a guide, we should have perished. The man that came for us brought two blankets, one for my wife, the other for Penelope: he desired us to be going. About a league distance from the place he left the canoe, which we parted with very unwillingly; for some of our people, had they had a mile further to have gone, could not have gone it. The wind still continued at northwest and blowed very fiercely; and extreme cold it was. We had such a continual

* "Sentinalls" in MS. copy.

shivering and pain in our bones that we were in violent anguish.

Our poor child was quiet, but so black with cold and shaking that it was admirable how it lived. We got to Augustine about two hours before night; being put on shore, we were directed to the governor's house: being got thither we were got up a pair of stairs, at the head whereof stood the governor, who ordered my wife to be conducted to his wife's apartment. I and John Smith went into a room where the governor asked us a few questions; but seeing how extreme cold we were, he gave us a cup of Spanish wine and sent us into his kitchen to warm ourselves at the fire. About half an hour afterwards the governor sent for John Smith and me and gave us a shirt and sliders, a hat and a pair of silk stockings, telling us he had no woollen clothes as yet, but would have some made. We put on the linen and made all haste into the kitchen to the fire. Robert Barrow was quartered at another house. The persons came to the governor's house and took such as they were minded to quarter in their houses; so that Joseph Kirle, John Smith, I, my wife and child lodged at the governor's house. All our people that came up with Joseph Kirle came to see us. We perceived the people's great kindness; for they were all well clothed from head to foot with the best the people had. Joseph Kirle began to tell us of his travail after he had left us on the bay, and how that they all concluded that they should never see my wife and child and Robert Barrow any more, if they did my kinsman and me. Richard Limpeney and those that went with him had a hard travel for thirty-six hours without ceasing, in which travel three of our Negroes that went with them were lost (viz Jack, Caesar, and Quenza), by sitting down to rest themselves they were in a little time so numbed that they could not go, and there perished. So that we lost five in that day's travel, and began to doubt that Negro Ben perished also. Joseph Kirle said that he thought he should have lost some of our people in their travel from the last sentinel's hither, for they were much tired, and the cold violent and the latter part of that day's journey they wading for many miles through much water, and deep sand-hills, and when they came in sight of Augustine they stayed for boats to fetch them, in which time some were numbed with the cold. Joseph Kirle applied himself to the governor on our behalfs to send us help, for he doubted whether we were all living; the governor readily assented and forthwith sent for a person fit for his purpose; charging him to get a piragua and men, and go forthwith and fetch us, but the tide fell out, so that we* could not go till midnight. The governor was so concerned that he would not go to bed till they were gone; when the tide served he went to the waterside and saw the men put off, giving them a strict charge.

Solomon Cresson began to tell us of his travels from Jece, having most part of the way much rain. The Indians were very kind unto him until they came to the Indian town where the Dutchmen were killed; at which place some of those Indians made a discovery of him to be no Spaniard. They said nothing to him thereof, but were very dogged to him, giving him no food, and causing him to lie on the ground amongst vermin. On the morrow he was to go with his former company; who were grown so extremely bitter and envious to him that when they did but look upon him, they were ready to smite him; having gone until about mid-day, passing an inlet, the weather being extreme bad with wind, rain and much cold, they put on shore; (this was the place where we put on shore and got water-soldiers and stayed for the Spaniard when he went back to look for our people that were to follow us in a canoe). But the rage of these bloody people was such that he expected to die; being on shore they readily kindled a fire, about which time he heard a noise of a boat and oars, and presently the Spanish piragua put on shore upon them. The Indians were extraordinarily surprised and stood amazed but Solomon was glad to see them, and they him: the Spaniards took the Old Cassee-key's chest and whatever he had from him, commanding them to return to the Indian towns from which they came. Staying all night the next morning the Spaniards sent Solomon under

* "They" in MS. copy.

the conduct of two Indians belonging to these towns who were commanded by the Spaniards to carry Solomon unto the sentinel's house, but these two Indians carried him a little beyond the place where we put on shore to travel, and they seemed as though they had mischief in their hearts against him: he asked if they would go forward? But they looking untowardly on him, answered him not: so he went himself and was glad when he saw they did not follow him.

But we were desirous to know how the Spaniards had knowledge of us which it seems was thus.

When we got to Jece where Smith and his company were, and we going under the denomination of Spaniards and the other English, the report of us run from Indian town to Indian town to the northward unto the northermost town, at which town were two or more Indians that were converted to the Romish faith. These or one of these went to the next Spanish sentinel's and gave an account that he heard that there were two vessels cast away to the southward of Jece, one being a Spaniard and the other an English vessel. The Spaniards having two vessels gone for the Havana to seek for supplies, feared it was those vessels. And the same day as this news came to the governor of Augustine came also news of one of their friars being murdered by some of the Cape Indians. After this manner we understood it; viz. three friars being under a vow to go amongst the Indians on the Cape to convert them, they went to a certain town to the northward of where we were cast away, but it lay within the sound. The Casseekey of this town they gained on to embrace the Roman faith, but all his people were much incensed against the friars, and therefore would have their Casseekey renounce his faith, and put the friars to death; but he would assent to neither: therefore they killed him and one friar; the other two escaped. Herewith was a piragua forthwith sent for us of what nation soever we might be, also a party of Spaniards and Indians were sent against that town where the friar was killed. We had a plentiful supper, and we fed like people that had been half starved, for we eat not knowing when we had enough:

and we found our palates so changed by eating of berries that we could not relish the taste of salt any more than if it had no saltness in it. We had lodging provided, but few beds.

The 9 month, 16; the 2 of the week.

This morning we had ice half an inch thick, and it had been so for some mornings past, but as the sun riseth it's gone.

The governor came this morning to our apartment, inquiring how we did? We having had chocolatta for breakfast he asked if we would have anything else that his house could afford: if we would but ask it would be brought us. But we modestly answered that this was sufficient although our appetites were not to be satisfied. The governor stated the poverty of the country unto us. The place is a garrison maintained one half by the King of Spain, the other half by the Church of Rome. The male inhabitants are all soldiers, every one receiving pay according to their post. A sentinel's pay is 150 pieces of eight a year. And all their supply of bread, clothing and money comes from the Havana and Porto Vella.* And it is a going on of three years since they have had a vessel from any place whatsoever, which makes their wants very great: all things being expended except ammunition and salt, of which they said they had enough. The governor offered us the freedom of what his house afforded, withal gave us a charge to be careful in going abroad, especially of some persons that did not affect our nation: we promised to be ruled and submit to the governor's pleasure for our liberty. Our people came in and we told them the caution; but they said they had been all over the town and in many houses where they were kindly received, and such as the people had they would give them. They told us of some English that lived here, and they had been at their houses; the chiefest in esteem was one William Carr of the Isle of Man, who about thirty years ago was in a vessel bound for South Carolina, but missing their port were cast away nigh this port, many were drowned, but he and some others were brought hither by the Indians, some of them

* Presumably, Porto Bello.

got away in Spanish vessels, others died here. This man turned Roman Catholic and married a Spanish woman, of whom he had seven children, and is an officer in the garrison. He was chief interpreter.

[*9 mo: 17th: 3*] This day came Joseph Kirle's Negro Ben. He gave us this account that after we had sent him back, he having looked and not finding my kinsman went to seek for a place to shelter himself from the cold, and some place he found to creep in where he lay down and continued there all night, but by morning was so stiff with cold that he could not use his legs, but hauled himself towards the bay. The Spaniard our guide from the first sentry house the morning after we went thence returned along the bay to see if any of our people were living, but he found all dead except Negro Ben, and he getting a fire made, Negro Ben was recovered and got the use of his limbs.

William Carr the interpreter acquainted us that the governor and two royal officers would examine us concerning our being cast away and what goods and moneys was lost in our vessel, and concerning our hardships amongst the Florida Indians &c., which was done, and everyone did sign it. This took up 2 or 3 days' time to complete it. After this was done the governor told us, that he expected Capt. Sebastian Lopez in some few days, and after his arrival he would provide for our going to Carolina with canoes and men to guard us.

This week my wife was taken with a fever and ague which held her three days and then left her. The governor ordered his own doctor to administer such things as were helpful. The governor's kindness to us all was extraordinary, for he would daily inquire of us if we wanted anything which he had, of which he gave us an account, and we eat no worse than he did daily.

The town we saw from one end to the other. It is about three quarters of a mile in length, not regularly built, the houses not very thick; they having large orchards, in which are plenty of oranges, lemons, pome-citrons, limes, figs and peaches: the houses most of them old building and not half of them inhabited. The number of men being about three hundred that belong to the government and many of them are kept as sentinels at their look-outs. At the north end of the town standeth a large fortification, being a quadrangle with bastions, each bastion will contain thirteen guns; but there is not passing two thirds of fifty-two mounted. In the curtain they cannot mount any guns being only for small arms. The wall of the fortification is about thirty foot high built of sawed stone, such as they get out of the sand between the sea and the sound. This stone is only sand and small shells connexed together being not very hard till exposed to the sun. The fort is moated round, they would not admit us to come near the fort: but Joseph Kirle took an opportunity and walked round about it.

The 9 month, 23; the 2 of the week.

This day Joseph Kirle and I considering that the latter end of this week was talked of for our setting forward towards Carolina (which the Spaniards call St. Georges,) we concluded to endeavor to provide ourselves, if we could, with clothing; considering we should be exposed to all the weather that might happen, and have no shelter but what we carried with us. Therefore we were inclined to sell, he his and I one or two of my Negroes to provide us clothing and provisions. We addressed ourselves to the governor and withal offered him if he pleased to accept the choice of my Negroes; but he denied our offer. We stated our matter to him and asked if we might dispose of our Negroes? He said, No, we should not, neither could we sell them to any person but himself for the king's account without a special license. Therefore he would consult the two royal officers and give us his answer.

The 9 month, 24; the 3 of the week.

This day the governor sent for us, and told us, that he would give us credit for what we and the rest of the company would. I told him that my wife and child would want some warmer clothing, also Joseph Kirle and myself should want some if to be had. He ordered us to give in an account of what we should want, and if to be had, he would get it. And Joseph Kirle and I should give our obligation to pay the governor of Carolina what the sum amounted unto; which we were willing to do. But we desired that our people should give us their obligation for what we were engaged for on their account; which the governor thought reasonable. I gave in an account of particulars for Joseph Kirle, Robert Barrow, myself and family: also the quantity of Indian corn, peas, stringed beef, salt and earthen pots for the whole company. But clothing was not to be had except as much stuff as made a suit for my wife and child, and a few skins Joseph Kirle and I got. I got also seven blankets though the price was great. These served Joseph Kirle, Robert Barrow, myself and family. We had five roves of ammunition, bread, so full of weevil that corn was far better. Twenty roves of strung beef: sixty roves of Indian corn, ten roves of peas, one rove of salt, jars for water, and earthen pots to boil our victuals in.

The 9 month, 25; the 4 of the week.

The governor sent for Joseph Kirle and me to certify that all that was to be got he had got for us. And he further signified unto us that we did expect Sebastian Lopez before this time, and he would not have us to go till he came, for whatever he could get of our money and goods we should receive it every doit. But we said we desired not to be detained on that account, for we had given that already over for gone from us. And as it had pleased God to make them the instruments of our preservation, so we did freely give any thing of that which was or may be deemed ours to the governor and those persons that were sent for us. The governor said he would not have anything to do with it, for whatever he did was for Charity's sake. Then we desired the soldiers should have it if anything should be got, which we doubted. And hereupon we considered that should those poor men get nothing we ought to allow them something in general; therefore Joseph Kirle and I offered the governor that we would allow Capt. Sebastian Lopez and his men an hundred pieces of eight for bringing us up from amongst the Indians. The governor was well pleased with our offer and said they should justly have it.

About this time Robert Barrow was taken with a grievous belly-ache, after which he fell into a violent flux. Several of our people also were taken with the belly-ache and great scouring, all which was chiefly occasioned by our unreasonable eating and not governing ourselves therein. Our chief diet was hominy, herbs and pumpions, having not much meat; which mean diet was our preservation. For had it been all flesh, we should have destroyed ourselves; but we had the best the place afforded.

The 9 month, 26; the 5 of the week.
This day we signed our obligation for four hundred pieces of eight, and we were to be gone the 28 or 29 instant, after which our people signed their obligation to us to pay their proportion of what was provided for them in provisions and their part of what should be paid for their passage from the Indians to Carolina. Whereupon we made the best provision we could: I had got some wine and brandy for myself and family and some small necessaries for our child, with a great resolution to go through.

The 9 month, 29; the 1 of the week.
This day after we had dined, canoes being got ready, one Capt. Francisco De Roma with six soldiers was to go our conduct; the governor walked down to see us embark, and taking our farewell he embraced some of us and wished us well, saying, WE SHOULD FORGET HIM WHEN WE GOT AMONGST OUR OWN NATION, and also added THAT IF WE FORGOT, GOD WOULD NOT FORGET HIM. Thus in a courteous manner we parted; which was about two or three o'clock in the afternoon. Taking our departure from Augustine, we had about two or three leagues to an Indian town called Sta. Cruce, where being landed we were directed to the Indian war-house: it is built round having sixteen squares; on each square is a cabin built and painted which will hold two people; the house being about fifty foot diameter. In

the middle of the top is a square opening about fifteen foot. This house was very clean, and fires being ready made nigh our cabins. The Spanish captain made choice of cabins for him and his soldiers and appointed us our cabins. In this town they have a friar and a large house to worship in with three bells, and the Indians go as constantly to their devotion at all times and seasons as any of the Spaniards. Night being come and the time of their devotion over, the friar came in and many of the Indians both men and women having a dance according to their way and custom. We had plenty of casseena drink and such victuals as the Indians had provided for us, some bringing corn boiled, another peas, some one thing, some another, of all which we made a good supper and slept till morning.

The 9 month, 30; the 2 of the week.

This morning early we left this town having about two leagues to go with the canoes, then we were to travel by land: but a cart was provided to carry our provisions and necessaries; in which cart those that could not travel were carried. We had about five leagues to a sentinel's house, where we lay all night, and next morning traveled along the seashore about four leagues to an inlet. Here we waited for canoes to come for us to carry us about two miles to a town called St. Wans, an Indian town, being on an island. We went through a kirt of wood into the Indian plantations for a mile. In the middle of this island is the town of St. Wans, a large town and many people. They have a friar and a worshipping house: the people are very industrious, having plenty of hogs and fowls and large crops of corn, as we could tell by their corn-houses. The Indians brought us victuals as at the last town, and we lay in their war-house, which was larger than that at the other town.

The 10 month, 2; the 4 of the week.

This morning the Indians brought us victuals for breakfast, and the friar gave my wife some loaves of bread made of Indian corn, which was somewhat extraordinary: also a parcel of fowls.

About ten o'clock in the forenoon we left St. Wans, walking about a mile to the sound where were canoes and Indians ready to transport us to the next town. We did believe that we might have come all the way along the sound, but the Spaniards were not willing to discover the place unto us.

An hour before sunset we got to the town called St. Mary's. This is a frontier and a garrison town: the inhabitants are Indians with some Spanish soldiers. We were conducted to the war-house, as the custom is, for every town hath a war-house. Or as we understood these houses were for their times of mirth and dancing, and to lodge and entertain strangers. This house is about 81 foot diameter built round, with 32 squares, in each square a cabin about 8 foot long of a good height being painted and well matted. The center of this building is a quadrangle of 20 foot being open at top of the house, against which the house is built thus.* In this quadrangle is the place they dance having a great fire in the middle. One of the squares of this building is the gateway or passage in. The women natives of these towns clothe themselves with the moss of trees, making gowns and petticoats thereof which at a distance or in the night look very neat. The Indian boys we saw were kept to school in the church, the friar being their schoolmaster. This is the largest town of all. About a mile from this is another town called St. Philips. At this town of St. Mary's were we to stay till the 5th or 6th instant; where also we were to receive our sixty roves of corn, and ten roves of peas; while we stayed we had one half of our corn beaten into meal by the Indians, the other we kept whole, not knowing what weather we should have: for the friar of this town some years past was at Charles Town in South Carolina, and he had a month's passage in going about at this time of the year. This news was very unpleasant to think of lying out a month at this season, having been so weather beaten before; but we endeavored to shun looking back, considering how great our preservations had been hitherto.

* The MS. copy reads: "being open at top of the house against which is built two."

While we stayed here we were willing to make all the provision we could for back and belly. We got of the Indians plenty of garlic and long pepper to season our corn and peas, both which were griping and windy: and we made us wooden trays and spoons to eat with; we got rushes and made a sort of platted rope thereof; the use we chiefly intended it for was to be serviceable to help us in building huts or tents with at such time as we should meet with hard weather.

The time drawing on that we were to leave this town, we had seven large canoes provided to carry us being in all about sixty persons; eighteen of us and 6 of Smith's company, seven Spaniards and thirty odd Indians, which were to row the canoes and be our pilots. We had some Indians from all the towns and two Casseekeys.

We understood that the Carolina Indians called the Yammasees, which are related to these Indians were here about a month since trading for deerskins.

I have omitted a considerable passage that happened in Augustine; the woman named Penelope being big with child, by the Spaniard's persuasion stayed with them. Also Joseph Kirle's boy named John Hilliar, was detained by the Spaniards. Joseph Kirle strove hard with the governor that he might have his boy; but the lad was conveyed out of town and not to be found. The governor promised that he would send him after him if possible; but the boy came not to us, and we were to depart hence on the morrow.

The 10 month, 6; the 1 of the week.

This morning we embarked and departed this place and put in to the town St. Philips where the Spanish captain invited us on shore to drink casseena, which we did. The Spaniards having left something behind, we stayed here about an hour and then set forward. About two or three leagues hence we came in sight of an Indian town called Sappataw; but we went about a league to the northward of it to a sentinel's house, where we put our boats on shore and had casseena brought us. Making no stay we went hence rowing till next morning: in the night we had lost our way, but got to rights in a little time.

The 7; the 2 of the week.

This morning we put on shore having passed an inlet of the sea, and here we dressed some victuals and got a little sleep until the tide served. Some of our Indians went out a-hunting for deer and hogs of both which the Spaniards said there was plenty, and when the tide served we were to go to the northermost end of this island and stay for the hunters. One of the Indians brought a deer which he throwed down amongst the other Indians, and he went out again to hunt to the north end of the island, where we were to rendevous for this night. We set forward about ten o'clock and got to the place appointed an hour or two before sunset, it being a fine lofty wood. We employed ourselves in getting firewood for the night and moss to lie on, of both which we got plenty, having a large oak to lie under.

The Indians brought in several hogs and deer, of which we had part, so that we fared richly; having a pleasant night's repose; we got up to be gone about an hour before day.

The 10 month, 8; the 3 of the week.

This day having rowed from the last place until two hours before sunset we put on shore at a place where had been an Indian settlement; it being on a high bank, from whence we had a prospect of the sound. Here we employed ourselves to go and fetch bushes to make shelter against the wind and dews of the night, and in cutting of dry grass to lie on, and getting of wood which was at considerable distance. But we resolved to have it if labor would purchase it. Those that were not employed in these services were providing of water and victuals, for we had always enough to do. We had a pleasant night and rested well.

The 10 month, 9; the 4 of the week.

This morning about sun-rising we saw a canoe of Carolina Indians agoing to the southward a-hunting: they kept the western side of the sound, being fearful of us. We had a canoe manned with Indians and Spaniards to go after them to speak with them, being desirous to get them to carry letters to inform of our coming, not knowing but we might alarm the out-settlement of Carolina.

This canoe of ours pursued the other, but the Carolina Indians put on shore, run into a marsh and fired at our people. The Spanish Indians who could speak the Yammaw's language, called unto them, and told them their business, withal entreating them to come unto them; but they answered that they were going a-hunting for the season, therefore desired them to be gone, for they would not come near them: thus our people returned unto us. The Carolina Indians went their way, and we prepared to go forward. We having the Casseekey of St. Wans with us sent him away last night, to see if he could meet any of the Yammasee Indians of Carolina, he being acquainted with and related to them: but this canoe passed him, we set forward and rowed all the day till about an hour before sunset, and then we put on shore at an Indian field which was overgrown with sedge, it being low wet land. Here we made our accustomed provision for lodging, lying this night in a wood, having dressed victuals for this time and tomorrow; and having rested well this night, about day-break or sooner we left this place.

The 10 month, 10; the 5 of the week.

This day about ten o'clock we crossed an inlet, but the tide being against us we put on shore at an old Indian field. At this place under the shelter of some trees was the Casseekey of St. Wans. Here we stayed and drank some casseena. There was abundance of rabbits, but we made no stay. Not passing two hours, the Casseekey was sent before to make discovery, and we followed rowing until an hour before sunset, by which time we got to the place called St. Catalena, where hath been a great settlement of Indians, for the land hath been cleared for planting, for some miles distant. Here we met also the Casseekey, also a canoe of Carolina Indians being a man his wife and children having his dogs and other hunting implements for to lie out this winter season. The Spanish captain by this interpreter discoursed him about carrying our letters, which he readily assented unto; whereupon the Spanish captain set himself to writing to the governor of Carolina.

We had a large field to lie in and no manner of shelter but what was a mile distant or more; but we spared not pains, but some fell to cutting of boughs and brush at that great distance, some to carrying it to the place, some to get firewood; so that by night we had a brave shelter.

The Spanish captain sent for me to write to the governor of Carolina; which I did. I writ also to a person of my acquaintance there. The letters being finished and night come on I delivered my letters to the captain and returned to my company. By this time they had completed our booth which we thought was sufficient, if no rain fell. We provided our victuals for our supper and for the next day's travel, as also some dry grass to lie on in hopes of resting well this night. About ten at night the Carolina Indians went with our letters for Carolina.

The 10 month, 11; the 6 of the week.

This morning about two hours before day we had a gust of wind at the northwest and the sky was overcast and looked as though we should have abundance of rain. In a little time the rain fell against which we had no shelter, but our blankets. The rain held until break of day, at which time began the northwest wind to blow violent hard and cold. Our shelter was fronting the northwest; and we fell to work to shift our booth and to getting more boughs, brush and grass: the grass was to fill and keep up a bank of earth which we raised about three or four foot high to break the wind from us. All this day were we employed in enlarging our booth and getting of wood for firing. The northwest blew extreme hard and this night was hard, getting but little rest, the cold pinching us.

The 10 month, 12; the 7 of the week.

This day the wind continued without ceasing. We began to mend what the wind had put out of order by night, and heaved up more earth on our booth, and made some enlargement, for we were not negligent by day to provide for the

night, which pinched us with cold especially aged Robert
Barrow, who having a violent flux that had held him from
Augustine hither, and by the violent cold being grown on him
so that he could not govern his weakness, nor get natural rest;
he was extremely racked with the cold, that in this juncture
of hardship we could get no warmth in him; but he was con-
tented with our mean help although he received little benefit
by it. This day at times we went out to get wood, having a
long way to go in an open field and the cold almost numbing
us by that time we could get to our booth. This evening the
wind was somewhat abated and we were in great hopes it was
over, but it blowed fiercely the latter part of the night.

The 10 month, 13; the 1 of the week.
This morning the wind was something abated and the sun
gave forth a little warmth: Joseph Kirle borrowed a gun,
powder and shot of the Spaniards, and went to kill some wild
geese or what other game he might come up with, but he had
no success, coming home without any game: and we were well
content with a dinner of Indian corn and strung beef. The
Spanish Indian hunted all these three days and killed several
deer, but they eat them as fast as they killed them; having
little or no other provision, their corn being spent.

The latter part of this day the wind was very moderate and
we hoped to be going the next morning. Whereupon we provided for the next day's travel.

The 10 month, 14; the 2 of the week.
This morning we embarked and set forward having fair
weather, the wind down: we rowed all day until three o'clock,
being come to a great inlet of the sea; but the weather looked
as though we should have wind and rain, and to cross the inlet
would be dangerous, it being about two leagues over, and a
little wind maketh a rough sea: so we put on shore, it being
high land and lofty woods, mostly pine and live oaks: here
we made all the expedition we could to get a shelter against
the weather. The Indians set to work to build themselves little
huts or wigwams, which they had not done till now. They got

small palmetto leaves and covered their buildings; but ours were covered mostly with boughs, which would not keep out much rain. By night we had a great deal of rain and wind. And it being the evening of the Spaniards' Christmas they used some of their ceremonies with tinkling on a piece of iron, and singing, begging for somewhat for the day following. They begged of the Indians, and the Indians in like manner begged of the Spaniards, and what the Indians gave the Spaniards, that was returned to the Indians.

The 10 month, 16; the 4 of the week.

This morning was very foggy and proved a rainy day, but we kept rowing until two in the afternoon, the rain being hard and the wind increased at N E. We put on shore, but the capt. told us we should not stay here long, he intended further, and if the weather permitted, would go all night; but the weather was likelier to be worse than better, and we sat in the rain until night was come. Then we entreated the captain that we might stay all night, and that we might provide against the weather; but he pretended the weather would break up and he would be gone. But there was no likelihood of it. The rain was increased and we all wet and shramed with cold; at length he assented to stay; then we were hard put to it (being night) to provide shelter: but in the dark did we work until we had made us a shelter that would keep the rain from us; having fires we put off our wet clothes and dried them as well as we could. Towards morning the rain broke up.

The 10 month, 17; the 5 of the week.

This morning at sun-rising we set forward and rowed until noon; at which time we came to an inlet and put ashore. There we stayed all this afternoon and dried our blankets and what was not dried last night. We also dressed victuals, and as soon as it was dark went hence designing to row all night, but having an intricate passage amongst marshes, where were divers creeks and ways, that we rowed sometimes in a wrong one, then back again, and rowed in another; and about midnight our pilots were at a loss not knowing which way to go, nor where to find any dry land that we might go on shore. But three of our boats rowed until we found a dry nap to get on shore, where we lay until day, having good fires. As soon as it was light we got our boats and went to look for the rest of our company whom we found having made their canoes fast to the sedge and sitting therein until we came to them.

The 10 month, 18; the 6 of the week.

The night was extreme foggy, and so was this morning; but we searched about and found our passage, being a little channel just broad enough for our boats to pass, and a mile in length. After we passed this, we came into a great sound which went down into a large inlet that the land could not be seen from the one side to the other. Into the sound comes down a great river called the Sabina River, which we got into the course of it, the water was fresh though in this great sound. The Spaniards called it the Cross Bar, or Sta. Cruce. About noon we got over this sound, and here we rowed out to sea for two leagues to get into another sound; and about three o'clock the wind began to blow at northeast, and it looked very black, so that we feared a storm. We desired to get on shore to provide against it, but the captain said, about a few leagues further we should get near Port Royal, but in the interim we saw a canoe on the shore. We made to her, and there we found some Indian wigwams. Here we went on shore. This was a canoe laden with skins that belonged to merchants at Carolina, having four Indians belonging to her; but three of them run away fearing the Spaniards, and one stayed.

The Indians' wigwams were in a bad condition not fit to keep out the weather; so we set to work to mend them. Here was plenty of palmetto leaves with which we covered them, and made addition to them, but the storm of wind and rain came violently before we could complete our work and held all night, yet we lay indifferent dry though the storm was very great.

The 10 month, 19; the 7 of the week.

This morning the storm of wind continued at NE. with

rain; we being likely to stay some time here enlarged our wigwam fearing a northwester, which about ten o'clock this day
began to blow fiercely with snow for some hours. The wind
was so violent that we feared lest the tall pines should be
blown on us. We sent the Carolina Indian out to bring his
three mates in; but they would not. The Spanish Indians
made great complaint for food. We gave amongst them four
rove of corn, not being willing to spare any more, not knowing
how long we should be detained by the weather. Some of our
people had almost eaten up their shares, and we expected,
should we be detained long, we must supply them with what
we had to spare.

The 10 month, 20; the 1 of the week.

This day the wind continued at **NW.** and extreme cold it
was, but we in our wigwam were well enough secured from
cold. About noon our mariners' wigwam got fire and was
burnt; theirs was the leewardmost of all (for we had eight
wigwams) otherwise the whole had been in danger. We
understood that we were not passing two or three days' journey from the English settlements; but the Spanish Indians
told us that it was more till we were better informed by this
Indian who belonged to that place.

The 10 month, 21.

This day early we set forward and passed Port Royal
sound, being some leagues over; and about two o'clock in the
afternoon we put on shore, the tide being against us. Here was
a close wood where we lay indifferent well all night, and early
in the morning we set forward and rowed all day until one
o'clock in the afternoon of the 22 day. At which time we got
to the first settlement in Carolina, belonging to one Richard
Bennet, who received us kindly, and provided plentifully for
us of good food and good drink, showing the Spaniards all
kindness possible he could for our sakes, which the Spaniards
did acknowledge. We stayed here all night.

The 10 month, 23.

This morning having eaten plentifully, and drank also, we

went hence in company of some of the inhabitants about ten o'clock, and rowed until two hours within night, having passed by several plantations. We put on shore on a point of land to wait a tide, having a wood to shelter in and making good fires we stayed until midnight, at which time we went thence and rowed until an hour or two before day, by which time we got to Governor Blake's house.

24. This morning when the governor arose he sent for Jo. Kirle, John Smith, Andrew Murray and me making inquiry of us concerning our passage and on what account the Spaniards came with us. We rendered him an account of the governor of Augustine's generosity towards us, and that he sent us freely without any demands except what we had freely contracted. The governor sent for the Spanish captain in, and received the letters that were sent from the governor of Augustine, also our obligation, which the governor accepted. The governor showed a great deal of kindness towards us, made inquiry into all our conditions. Robert Barrow he sent to his neighbor Margaret Bammer's, who, he said, would be careful and nurse him: she was an ancient Friend, about 2 miles distant; so he went on horseback. The governor clothed Jos. Kirle, John Smith, Andrew Murray; me, my wife and child. To the rest of our people he gave each of them a duffle blanket which would keep them warm: and plenty of victuals and drink was provided. We obtained leave of the governor to permit the Spaniards to go to Charles Town with us being willing to gratify them according to our abilities.

The 10 month, 25; the 6 of the week.
This day in the afternoon, Joseph Kirle, John Smith, I, my wife and child went to Margaret Bammer's where Robert Barrow was; staying all night till next morning, when the Spaniards called for us as they came by water.

26. This morning we went hence with the Spaniards for Charles Town, where we arrived about an hour within night.
The gentlemen of the town appointed a public house of good credit to entertain the Spaniards with meat and drink

and lodging; which was done to the Spaniards' admiration; they stayed here 8 days. We got our people together and agreed jointly to give the Spaniards 100 pieces of 8, which Jo. Kirle and I divided amongst them according to their degrees, we two adding to the sum.

The 11 month, 4; the 2 of the week.

Joseph Kirle and I provided a small present to send to the governor of Augustine, and this day we went with the Spaniards to Governor Blake's, staying there one day; the governor treated the Spaniards, and having completed his letters gave the Spanish captain a considerable present and sent him homewards, ordering them to call on the Yammassee Indians, where they might have as much Indian corn, as they pleased, to carry home with them, the towns of these Indians being about two or three days' rowing from Charles Town.

The 11 month, the 9; the 7 of the week.

This day I returned with my wife and child to Charles Town, leaving Robert Barrow in a weak and low condition with Margaret Bammer. I, my wife and family with Joseph Kirle were entertained by Captain James Ribee the time of our stay in Carolina. Our seamen were mostly employed, some in one vessel, and some in another that belonged to the port.

The 12 month, 6; the 2 of the week.

Joseph Kirle went hence to the island of Providence in hopes of gaining speedy passage for Pennsylvania the place of his abode.

Towards the beginning of this month Robert Barrow was brought to Charles Town being extreme weak and was lodged at the house of Mary Cross who nursed him.

The 1 month, 18; the 5 of the week.

This day I with my family and Robert Barrow embarked and set sail from this place for Pennsylvania, and had fourteen days' passage to Philadelphia.

The 2 month, 4; the 1 of the week.

This day in the evening Robert Barrow departed this life

and was buried the 6 instant having passed through great exercises in much patience; and in all the times of our greatest troubles was ready to counsel us to patience and to wait what the Lord our God would bring to pass. And he would often express that it was his belief, that our lives should be spared not be lost in that wilderness and amongst those people who would have made a prey of us. And so this good man having finished his course with joy laid down his body, and is with Him who rewards the just.

Thus having completed our hard passage hither, wherein God's great mercy and wonderful loving kindness hath been largely extended unto us in delivering and preserving us to this day and time, I hope that I with all those of us that have been spared hitherto, shall never be forgetful nor unmindful of the low estate we were brought into; but that we may double our diligence in serving thee, Lord God, is the breathing and earnest desire of my soul. Amen.

JONATHAN DICKINSON.

Appendices

APPENDIX A

The Preface to the *Journal*, 1699
[author unknown]

INGRATITUDE towards men, after signal favors received, is, amongst all civilized people, looked upon with a just detestation: insomuch that the moral Gentiles in ages past, thought they could give no worse a character of a person than to call him ungrateful. How much more then are Christians (especially in a time of such light, as now shineth) engaged, to shun this sin of ingratitude, towards their God, whom they sensibly know, to be the Fountain of all their mercies. And surely, next to the infinite mercy showed them for Christ's sake, in causing the day-spring from on high to visit their souls, remarkable outward deliverances, ought in a more than commonly remarkable manner, to be the objects of their gratitude, to their great Deliverer. I must confess, thanksgiving (which is what we poor mortals can return for the manifold favors we daily receive from him) hath its rise in the heart; and as out of the abundance of the heart the mouth speaketh, how can those who are truly thankful in heart, but render the calves of their lips; in telling to their friends and acquaintance, how great things God hath done for them. Nay, they are so affected, with such eminent appearances of the protecting hand of Providence, for their help, preservation and deliverance; that they are not willing to confine it to them only, but to publish it to the world; that the fame of their God may be spread from sea to sea, and from one end of the earth to the other.

The following relation being large, I shall endeavor to be short; only, some of the things which seem to me most remarkable I would more particularly recommend to the reader's observation.

1. *The hearts of all men are in the hand of God,* he can turn them as he pleases. When these man-eaters' fury was at height, their knives in one hand, and the poor shipwrecked people's heads in the other; their knees upon the others' shoulders, and their looks dismal; on a sudden, the savages were struck dumb, and their countenances changed, that they looked like another people; the Casseekey (or king) becoming as a safeguard to the distressed, from the injuries of his own men. Nay, such confidence he put in them, that he would trust them to remove the money he had taken from themselves, before he would trust his own. When they were got from these (people) to another place, where they expected more safety, they found themselves disappointed, fresh dangers preventing themselves, as dismally as before; yet God prevented any further mischief, than the stripping them of those poor rags the others had left them, and some other abuses, which by that time were grown familiar to them, and were looked upon as light afflictions. The Casseekey's wife being made an instrument for their delivery, she and some others having something of tenderness of heart in them, though amongst such an inhumane crew.

2. Many were the particular deliverances upon occasion of injuries offered. Once, an arrow shot at them narrowly escaped them. Another time, some going to shoot arrows at them, certain of their own company caught hold of their bows and arms; nay, though some of them shot, yet their arrows missed. Not to mention the frequent dangers they were in, upon every slight suspicion of their being English, of which more anon. And well might these poor sufferers be in continual fear of their lives, since about a 12-month before a parcel of Dutchmen who had likewise suffered shipwreck, had been killed and devoured; and moreover, of the many vessels supposed to be lost on that coast, these are the first company that are known to have escaped. Neither is it so wonderful that they are thus cruel to strangers, since they are unnatural to

their own aged people; they having no more compassion on them, than to make them slaves to the younger. Yet are these man-eaters as cowardly as cruel; when the Spaniards came up, the sight of a rusty musket presented towards them, would make several of them flee.

3. The dangers they were delivered from, arose not only from men, but the elements also God permitted to threaten them, and afflict them. One time rowing in their boat, the sea swelled, so that it was dangerous continuing thereon all night, and as dangerous, to endeavor for the shore; yet Providence failed them not, but conducted them safe thither, as though there had been a lane made through the breakers. Another time, by reason of a great flood, they were forced to remove their lodging several times, and for divers days, were in a continual apprehension of being drowned, at length were preserved upon an oyster hill. Not to mention the frequent dangers they were in, by reason of the extreme cold, too tedious to touch at here. Wherein this however is remarkable; that God can both administer strength in the midst of weakness, and also take away strength, and cause weakness to seize, whenever he pleases. Here was an old man, a woman with a sucking child, and another with child, persons, seemingly, very unlikely to encounter such hardships, all escaped, and divers Negroes, used to more hardiness, perished.

4. As to lodging; I shall say little, any discreet person may imagine, how hard it was to people well brought up, to lie on a floor, swarming with abundance of many sorts of creeping things, occasioned by the throwing the berry stones on the floor, and letting all the nastiness they made lie there, which bred these vermin; and yet perhaps might be accounted good lodging, in comparison of the cold ground, whereon they often lay afterwards unsheltered, exposed to the bleak blasts of the rigid northwest wind.

5. Their food mostly scanty, the best of it such, as (I am ready to think) the meanest Negro here would not touch with his lips: Sometimes the gills and guts of fish picked off a dunghill, sometimes the scraps the Indians flung away, and the

water they boiled their fish in, though never so undecently handled. At first their sorrows were so great, and their alarms so many, they could not eat; afterwards their diet so uncouth, they could not away with it; until at length hunger had so far prevailed over them, that they could eat with an appetite, the palmetto berries, the taste whereof was once irksome, and ready to take away their breath: nay, so fond were they of them, that the getting about a bushel accidentally, was looked on as a great prize.

6. Their being forced to mask themselves under the name of Spaniards though few of them could speak any Spanish, was another hardship: mostly because the natives often suspected them to be English, and thereby they were continually in danger of their lives. Whether their cruelty against the English, proceeds from their being under no apprehension of danger from them, and so may think themselves lawless, in what they do against our nation; or whether it proceeds, from any particular disgust offered them by some English, I shall not determine. However it would do well, for those that are not under their power, to avoid giving them any just cause of offense, lest their neighbors suffer for their faults. One of these savages could complain that, some years past, he had been taken off by some of our English sloops, from whom he had escaped by swimming, and was therewith disgusted, insomuch, that could he, by his sifting, have found out that they were English, it might have proved of ill consequence to them.

7. The courtesy of the governor of Augustine, who clothed these naked people, fed their hungry stomachs, and caused them to be conducted safely to Carolina, is not to be passed by without due notice; especially being a man of another nation, as well as of a different religion, and what is more, of such an one, as doth not teach its votaries, so much compassion, towards those they count heretics. Neither let me forget the governor of Carolina, whose generosity completed what the governor of Augustine had begun, in assisting and cherishing these our afflicted friends and country folks; with which I shall conclude

these remarks, to treat more particularly, concerning that faithful servant of the Lord, Robert Barrow, who was one of this company.

This man of God, whose habitation was in one of the northern counties of England, was early convinced of the blessed truth of God, professed by the people called Quakers, and soon after had a dispensation of the Gospel committed to him. He lived in his native country, in esteem amongst his neighbors, for his godly conversation, and honored in the Church of God, as an elder who had abode faithful in his testimony, both in preaching the Gospel, suffering for the same, and behaving himself answerably thereunto. And in the year 1694 the Spirit of God (from whom he first had his commission) requiring him to come over into these parts, to preach the Gospel here also; he was not disobedient to the heavenly call, but gave up to do the will of God, though in a cross to his own, as appeared by an expression of his, before he left England, which was to this effect, "That he had rather immediately have laid down his natural life there, if by so doing he could have kept his peace with God, than to have crossed the seas to America." Well! hither he came, and after he had throughly visited these parts, he took ship for the West Indian islands, and at length was returning from Jamaica, to this town of Philadelphia, when these calamities mentioned in the ensuing journal befell him. How he behaved himself under them, is therein expressed, with what patience he was carried through them, with what faith he overcame, even the very worst of men, so that it may be said, he was more than a conqueror over those bloodthirsty cannibals; looking to Him Who was invisible, and by His grace seeing beyond them and their cruelty; by prayer wrestling with God for a blessing, even the blessing of being delivered out of their barbarous hands, and laying his bones amongst faithful Friends; and so effectual were his fervent prayers, that they prevailed with God; and so gracious was his God unto him, that He sealed an assurance upon his spirit, that his prayers were heard, and should in due time be answered, before he was yet off his knees. And doubtless, he was made a strength and a comfort, to his companions in affliction, whose remembrance will not be easily blotted out of their minds.

One remarkable passage I cannot well omit, which demonstrates, he had well learnt of Him Who is a God of truth, to speak the truth upon all occasions though with the hazard of his life. For as the reader may observe in the series of this following relation, these poor people, for the safeguard of their lives, had assumed the name of Spaniards, some on that account asserting what was wrong, others concealing the trust, yet this honest-hearted man, being directly asked the question, *Nickaleer, Nickaleer?* (their word for Englishman) could do neither; but in simplicity answered, yes; being asked so concerning another, he again answered, yes. Yet, though for his plain dealing he was stripped of his clothes, which till then he had saved; God suffered not these savages to touch his life, or the lives of any of his company.

Thus he passed through this afflicting trial, and at length arrived at this place, on the 1st day of the 2d month 1697; though in much weakness, having been taken very ill of the belly-ache and flux at Augustine, of which he never recovered, but still grew worse and worse, to his dying day. It was about the 8th hour in the evening, when the barkentine he was passenger in, arrived at this place. Divers Friends went on board, in order to get him ashore, but he being in a very weak condition, they could not remove him at that time. He declared "his great satisfaction, that the Lord had granted his request, that he might lay down his bones in this place; that his heart was strong, and he hoped he might first see Friends again at the Meeting. He made mention of the goodness of God to him, and that His presence had attended him in all his exercises."

The next morning being the 2d of the 2d month, divers Friends went on board, to help the vessel up to a wharf, in order to get him on shore, in which time he spake as before related, God's power attending him. About the 7th hour, divers Friends carried him in a hammocker (being wrapt up in a blanket and cloths to keep him warm) to the house of Samuel Carpenter, where he declared "the goodness of God to him, and that his heart was yet strong, and his memory and understanding good"; after which he was shifted and then slept a considerable time.

Being awaked, he uttered at several times very comfortable and precious expressions, which some who were present, afterwards committed to writing, what they could remember, and are as follows. He inquiring what was become of George Keith's people? Was answered; that they were strangely divided, many of them become Baptists, and the honest-hearted amongst them returned to Friends. He said to this purpose, "They were split upon the Rock they had rejected. And that though it might please God yet to try us many ways, by suffering our neighboring governments to tempt or persuade us, to set up or establish the national ministry here; yet, he desired us, to stand in faithfulness against it, and not touch therewith. And he believed they would also much endeavor, to persuade us to join with them, in establishing and maintaining a militia amongst us; which he also desired us not to touch with, and that if we kept faithful to the Lord, He would defend and preserve us, and that we needed no such means of preservation for if our ways did please the Lord, He would make our enemies to be at peace with us." And he further said, "That Prophecy was fulfilled, and a remnant were witnesses of it. That swords should be beat into ploughshares, and spears into pruning-hooks; and that those who make use of the sword, should perish with the sword."

Speaking concerning some friends of the ministry in Old England, he said: "Many Friends about us that were rich men, and had public testimonies, were much cumbered with their worldly concerns, which was a great hindrance to their public service, and I would be often speaking to them about it. For (said he) I found it to be a hindrance to me, and so I gave it all up into my son's hands, he allowing me and my wife so much a year, and then I was at liberty, and had the world under my feet; which I would oft be telling them."

He often said, "That this place was God's plantation; that in Jamaica and Carolina there were but few Friends, but that this place had a great fame abroad, wherever he had been, for an honest, laborious and good people." Whereupon he exhorted us many times "to keep up our fame," and told us the means how "by being faithful to God, and keeping in love one with another and by forgiving our trespasses one against another": Often exhorting us to love one another, mentioning that expression of our Saviour, "By this shall all men know that ye are my disciples, if ye love one another." He likewise pressed us "to meet often together"; using this scripture as a motive thereto, "For they that feared the Lord met often together, and spake often one unto another, and a book of remembrance was written." He further said, "The Lord had given him the desire of his heart in coming hither, and that, if he died here, he was very well satisfied, and he believed his wife would also be well satisfied: and that as the Lord had given her to him, and him to her, so they had given one another up; and that when he came from her, it was as if he was going to his grave; that neither gold nor silver, riches nor honor, should have parted them, but that he did it only in obedience to the Lord, and to keep his peace with God."

He said, "that [he] had been convinced about forty-five years; and had borne a faithful testimony against the hireling priests, and had been in prison seven times for his testimony, and the Lord had always been his Preserver and Deliverer, by ways that he thought not of. And so Friends," said he, "will He be to you, if you be faithful to Him; and that several who had been committed prisoners with him, had used indirect means to get at liberty; but it was always my resolution," said he, "not to bow a knee to Baal; and yet the Lord wrought my deliverance." And further he said several times, "That in his late afflictions, he had seen more of the wonders and dealings of the Lord, than ever he had seen before, or ever should have seen, if he had not gone through them, and that he felt the Lord with him, which did out balance all."

Speaking of his patient bearing his sufferings, and how he

was supported by the Lord's power under all, and of his inquiry of the Lord about it, the Lord's answer was: LET PATIENCE HAVE ITS PERFECT WORK. Speaking how sick he was at Jamaica for about twenty weeks, "yet," said he, "I missed but one meeting." He also said, "that he desired of the Lord, that he might not die by the hands of those Barbarians; for," said he, "they thirsted, or longed as much after our flesh, as ever we did after victuals."

On the 3d day of the 2d month, some Friends coming into the room to visit him, at the sight of them he seemed to rejoice, and putting forth his hand, was ready to embrace them in much love, and in a very tender frame of spirit. The Friends expressed their gladness to see him, but said, they were sorry to see him so very weak; to which he replied, "Although my body be weak, my mind is sound, and memory good." And further said, "The Lord hath been very good to me, all along unto this very day, and this morning hath sweetly refreshed me." And further added, "The Lord hath answered my desire, for I desired content, and that I might come to this place, to lay my bones amongst you." And afterwards said, "It is a good thing, to have a conscience void of offence, both towards God, and towards man."

On the 4th day of the 2d month, being the 1st day of the week, about the 5th hour in the morning, he desired a Friend to write for him to his dear wife, "to remember his dear love to her, and to let her know of his travels, and being here, and that the Lord was with him; that his outward affairs were settled, and that she had wherewithal to live on." He further said, divers Friends being present, "That the Lord was with him, and all things were well, and that he had nothing to do, but to die." And accordingly on this day he departed, and on the 3d day following, being the 6th day of the 2d month, was buried in Friends burying ground, in this town of Philadelphia.

And now having brought my relation concerning this good man, to the last period of his life, I might very well here put a period to my preface; but that I foresee, some persons may be ready to say: here is an account of very strange passages, but of what credit is the relator? May we depend upon his authority, without danger of being imposed upon? To such I answer, He is a man well known in this town, of good credit and repute on whose fidelity and veracity, those who have any knowledge of him, will readily tell, without suspecting fallacy. But, that in the mouth of two or three witnesses everything may be established; besides him and his wife, a person whose residence (when at home) is in this town, viz. Joseph Kirle, the master of the barkentine in which they suffered shipwreck, a man of an honest character amongst his neighbors, had the perusal of it, before it went to the press, and approved of it. With which I shall conclude; wishing my reader much satisfaction in the reading of it: but never the unhappiness, of experiencing in proper person, the truth of it.

APPENDIX B

Letter from Robert Barrow to His Wife

WHILE Robert Barrow was resting at the Charleston home of Mary Cross, a fellow member of the Society of Friends, he wrote the first letter he had sent his wife Margaret since one written ten months before in Jamaica. It was also, so far as we know, the last he lived to send her. Barrow's account of his recent experience confirms Dickinson's journal in every important respect. It is reprinted from a Quaker journal, *The Friend, 85,* 278.

Ashley River in South Carolina the 23rd 12 mo. 1697.

Margaret Barrow my dear wife

Bossome Friend and Sister In the Faith and Fellowship of the Glorious Gospel Power. Well if thou be yet alive, thou may hereby know, that I am also alive in the body and also in the Truth of God, and Testimony of Jesus, blessed and praised be the God of my Life and Salvation.

And Dear Wife it is now long since I writt to thee and Frids, the last time it was last 2nd mo. wherein I gave you an account of Robert Wardells sickness death and Buriall. John and Rebecca Shaw, my dear children whom I dearly love and often remember when the lord Inlarges my heart and prepares my mind then I can and doe supplicate his Name on your behalfes praying for your Growth and prosperity, in the blessed Truth; and that you may educate your Children in the Way they should goe and be a good Example to them, remembering my dear love to all our dear Friends, of the Quarterly meeting of Westmoreland and Lancaster or any other that may enquire after me.

My dear Companion Robert Wardell lived in Jamaica but 15 days, but I lived 20 weeks and had not one dayes health, but soe burnt up with scorching heate of the Climate, I was always Thirsty and Feaverish. I had no stomach to meat, and

89

yet Travilled to again 200 miles, and kept Meetings; after gote to sea and was better intending for Pensilvania. We sailed along the Borders of Cuba and through the Gulph of Florida, and afterwards a great storme of Wind and Rain arose and drove us violently on shore on the Coast of Florida, and soe ship wracked; Tho' as it pleasd God all our lives were preserved from the Rage of the sea; Yet we came to be exposed to the hands of unreasonable men that hath no Faith, they are the Savage Indians and Barbarians known formerly to be men eaters these lookt upon us with arrogant & envious aspect being blood Thirstye and Envious in their hearts and we expected every moment to be murthered, some Indians were eager to doe it, and others of them were not, yet tho' their Treasure and Spoyle they had from our ship, wch was valued at 5000. pounds in Moneys and plate Gould and many sorts of Goods, nevertheless they fell on us to strip us of our cloathes—at first left us some Torne linen and some hats and shoes but we traveling on the sea coast as the Indians pleased to convey us, comeing to another coast, where abundance of Indians Men Women and Children gathered together to see us Murthered as we went: after that they had striped every one young and old as naked as when we came into the World, and gave them to the boys and Women, and when we were killed the Cloathes should not be blooded soe the Throng Crowded abo't us Naked people we were about 26 in number and one of them knockt a young man on the head, other stopped him, and some of them made away out of the crowd and put us from among them, and hastened us away upon the sea coast: I looked back and they were throng in dispute, some for a murder and some not, soe it pleased God to Divide them, and he gave us our life for a Prey, we were conveyed to the next Towne, and some of those Indians gave us Matts to sit on and gave us Fish to Eate, We had noe food for 3 days except Berrys and Wild Grapes and went naked without hat Cap Shirt or Coate stockings or shoes 7 weeks Time which was in the 7th 8 and 9th month the sun being Hot and scorching in the Dayes, and sometimes Rawe & great dewes fell in the

Night, that made Cold mornings; we being soe punished with
Muskeato Flyes; . . . mostly lyeing on the Ground either in
the Wigwams, or in the Woods, and the earth is all full of
Flyes and creeping things, in soe much that I gote no sleep nor
had no appetite to my meate, only thirsting after an extreame
manner. Well after a while the Governor of St. Augustine sent
a great Cannoe, near 20 Leagues to meet us of wch we were
glad, being sorely Tryed, when we came to this great Garrison
Towne, the Governor and most of the souldiers met us at the
shoare; and we were dismaile objects to look upon, he ordered
us all to come to his house, he gave order to the servants to
dress meat enough for us all in the meantime they gave every
one of Us a piece of Indian Corne Bread, oh I thought is was
the bravest that ever I had before, we having seen noe Bread
of any kind of Corne, for 7 weeks before, then he said to his
neighbors—I will lodge such and such soe took the Chiefest
of the company to lodge with him, and we were all disposed of
presently and they pull'd off the Raw buckskins, and gave us
such cloathes as they could spare, and there was one of the
Fathers a Confessor with his shaven Pate he sent me a linnin
shirt, so these Spanish Papists were kind to us, and after 2
weeks they sent us away; with a Captain and a Band of souldiers to the number of 26, well armed men, for there was a
wild sort of Indians between St. Augustine and Ashley River.
We had difficult going thither, and Wind and Tide against us
and lay mostly in the Woods, soe at Length we arrived at
Ashley River. And it pleased God I had a Great fortune to a
good nurse, one whose Name you have heard of, a Yorkshire
Woman born within Two miles of York her maiden Name was
Mary Fisher, she that spoke to the great Turke afterwards
Wm Bayly's Wife. She is now my Landlady and Nurse, only
she is a Widow of a second Husband her Name is now Mary
Cross.

Soe now I would not have my wife and Children of Frids
take thought of me, for tho' of late I have indured great hardship want and Nourishmt and help, yet now the God of my
life who hath borne my head in all distresses doth all along

provide for me suppose I must dye here 'twill not be for want of Necessaries or Good Providing I want for nothing that is fitt to be administered, neither food nor Phsysick, but I have a great want of sleep, I have been now about 13 weeks in this violent illness, some say there is noe Cure, let it be as pleases God I am content, the sting of Death hath been removed from Mee many Years agone, Glory to God who gives Faith and victory—Well Frids if I had not met with many obstructions since R. W. Dyed, I aimed to have been in England before this time, soe my near and dear Relatives with all my good Friends in Truth I bid you all farwell in the Lord, whether I have the opportunity to see you again or not, I shall remain your Friend and Brother whilst I am

ROBERT BARROW

I am tired with writing this Letter has been 3 days Work, I am become very Leane and poor of Body yet my heart is strong & the Lord my God beareth up my head and I have had a Meeting every first day and the Lords power and presence is not Wanting Glory to his name over all

APPENDIX C

The Florida Indians in the Seventeenth Century

THE Indian tribes of Florida in the seventeenth century (not including the Apalache) may be classified conveniently under five principal heads, each of which includes a number of smaller tribes, dominated by local caciques and all more or less racially and linguistically related. Southernmost of all were the Tegesta or Tequesta, a name variously spelled, that seems to be associated with a cacique, a village, and a group of tribes. As a group of tribes the Tequesta were a savage people, scattered up and down the eastern seaboard, in what is given on early maps, such as those of Visscher, 1700, Moll, 1710, and others of 1720 and 1723, as "Tegesta Province," extending from the Keys to a point considerably north of Cape Canaveral. On later maps, such as those of De Brahm, Jeffreys, and others "The Ancient Tegesta now Promontory of East Florida," "Ancient Tegesta," and "Old Tegesta" are all represented as lying south of the twentieth degree of northern latitude. Still later the name disappears altogether as designating a separate geographical province.

The Tequesta had been the object of a proselyting movement in the sixteenth century, when the Jesuits established a fortified mission on the site of the present Miami on Biscayne Bay, 1565–72, a mission that was abandoned in the latter year and not revived until the Franciscans renewed the attempt in 1743. Among the Tequesta tribes were the Viscaynos, from whom the name of Biscayne Island, Biscayne Bay, and Key Biscayne are supposed to be derived. Powerful in the seventeenth century, these tribes rapidly dwindled in numbers under the attacks of the Lower Creeks, who began their advance into Florida soon after the invasion of the peninsula by Captain James Moore of South Carolina in 1702 and 1703, and they were eventually absorbed, such of them as remained in southern Florida, into the Lower Creek group, all taking the name of

Seminoles (the "Wild People," or those intentionally holding aloof from the white man), somewhere about the middle or end of the eighteenth century.

West and southwest of the Tequesta, from the southernmost point of Florida to the vicinity of Tampa Bay on the west coast, were the Caloosa tribes, so called from their sixteenth century cacique, Calos or Carlos, who supposedly took his name from that of the emperor Charles V, king of Spain. Carlos and his son of the same name had their seat at San Antonio (Cape of Carlos, Bay of Carlos, Charlotte Bay, Harbor, or Haven, as it was variously called), and there it was that Captain Pedro Menéndez de Avilés, the Adelantado, visited him, had prolonged and intimate dealings with him (though each was mutually suspicious of the other), and eventually took his sister to wife, sending her off to Havana to be educated as a Christian. Carlos ruled over many lesser caciques and levied tribute from them, though he frequently had difficulty in maintaining his superior lordship over them. He was hostile to the Tequesta, who seem to have been friendly to the Spaniards, as Carlos was not, and though he had political dealings with the cacique at Biscayne Bay, the relations were never permanent, even though it is stated that at one time Tequesta was Carlos's vassal.

As with other Florida tribes the Caloosa soon ceased to exist as a separate people. In the eighteenth century they were gradually driven south to the more remote Keys and so reduced in numbers and importance that by 1835 (at the opening of the second Seminole War) there was but a remnant left. This remnant, as well as that of the Tequesta, was merged in the Seminoles, who had been driven from the north by the invading white settlers; and a part of the region once occupied by them became the southern reservation of the mixed-blood Seminole Indians. Of the language of the Caloosa nothing has survived except the names of some of their villages, though the name Caloosa itself is to be found in the Caloosahatchee, a river, the chief outlet of Lake Okeechobee, which flows into Charlotte Bay. There are no certain remains of their occupancy, except perhaps a few true kitchen middens, resulting from the gradual accumulation of refuse through many years of possession.

North of the Tequesta were the Indians with whom the Dickinson company came into contact during its distressing journey from Jupiter Inlet to St. Augustine, as narrated in the journal. The identification of these Indians, who by some writers are classed among the Tequesta (just as the latter, as well as the Ais, are rated by other writers as part of the Caloosa group), is far from certain as to either name or territory. Little is known about them to the student of the Indian ethnology of Florida, for no information, as far as the seventeenth century is concerned, can be obtained from Spanish sources and the Dickinson narrative is the only reliance. All of those tribes lying between Biscayne Bay and Cape Canaveral were loosely scattered, living chiefly along the coastal regions on the east, on the narrow islands behind the sand reefs, generally near the mouths of rivers, creeks, and inlets, for the interior was in many parts encumbered with tangled undergrowth, mangrove swamps, and salt marshes. The region from the Keys north to the lands south of Cape Canaveral was, geologically speaking, in all ways West Indian, similar in structure to the Bahamas themselves. There was no occupied back country in this part of Florida, just as there was none in the Bahama Islands. Life was centered in the lands away from the beaches, where were the Indian villages and where the Indians found in the sea and the inflowing rivers the scene of their chief activity. We know from the Dickinson narrative that the Indians possessed sea-going canoes, one of which had two masts and two sails, and from earlier accounts we learn of Indian canoes capable of holding thirty men. With these the Indians could go measurable distances out from the land into the ocean, from which they obtained an important part of their food supply. Despite their nearness to the coast and avoidance of the interior as unsuitable even for Indian use, it is probable that their villages and towns were, as a rule, invisible from the water. Jece, where the

95

shipwrecked company lived for more than a month, was half a mile from the sea, lying within the land along the sound and surrounded by a mangrove swamp, which hid the town from observation.

The tribes thus located north of the Tequesta were the Jobeses and two or three other tribes, to all of which have been given the name Jeagas or Jaegas, a name which may have come from the Spanish Rio Jega or Gega, found on Spanish maps of the seventeenth and eighteenth centuries (Blaeu, 1642, Visscher, 1700, and Liguera, 1742) at a point represented by Lake Worth Inlet. If so, then the name would seem to belong to a tribe south rather than north of Jupiter Inlet, as the map makers when not using Spanish terms were accustomed to name each river after the tribe living somewhere up the stream, for as a rule the Indians, when not dwelling along the banks of an inland water, located their villages on inlets opening into the ocean. These Jeagas or Jaegas may have been on the northern verge of the "Old Tegesta Province" and so be classifiable among the Tequesta, just as some writers have thought that the Jobeses and the tribes north to St. Lucie Inlet might also be characterized as Tequestas. Exactness and reliability in locating and labeling these Indian tribes is not possible in all cases, for the connections and relationships seem to have ebbed and flowed in such confusing fashion as to lead some anthropologists to adopt the practice of grouping together adjacent and apparently related tribes when the information was insufficient to make their separations clearly indicated. The Ais, whose name is well established, controlled the territory From St. Lucie Inlet to the waters behind Cape Canaveral.

North of the Ais were the Timucuas extending from Cape Canaveral to St. Augustine and beyond to the St. Mary's River. North of the Timucuas were the Guale, a small group living not in Florida but on the islands and part of the mainland of southeastern Georgia. The Guale have been classed as a subordinate tribe of the Yemassee, the Indians of South Carolina, with whom the English fought a bitter war in 1715, a war brought on not by the Indians but by the iniquities of the white traders. Probably there was a blood and language relationship between the Timucuas on the one hand and the Guale and the Yemassee on the other. Though the Dickinson narrative has mention of the Yemassee it says nothing of the Guale and contains no hint of their existence, unless we are to suppose, as was probably the case, that the company considered the Guale merely a Yemassee tribe.

The Indians that seized and maltreated the shipwrecked party were the Jobeses or dwellers on the Rio Jobe, as the Spaniards called what later came to be known first as Jupiter and later as Grenville Inlet. The name appears as "Rio Jobbe" on French and Spanish maps of the eighteenth century, and on the De Brahm map of 1770 the entry is "Grenville Inlet." But on an earlier De Brahm map, the date of which is uncertain, we find the name given as "Jupiter now Grenville," showing that Jupiter was an older form than Grenville, and oddly enough on Purcell's map of 1783 appears "Rio Job or Grenville River," showing a persistence of the Spanish form. In any case the name Jupiter was used long before the "Celestial Railroad" came into existence, the Olympian names of whose stations—Neptune, Venus, Mars, and Juno—owe their origin to the preëxisting example of Jupiter and not vice versa. This leaves the origin of the name Jupiter still in doubt. Has it any connection with the Spansh Jobe by way of an English rendering? Excellent authorities think that it has, for on a Spanish map of 1742 we find the River Jobe entered as "Jove" (*Plano dela Costa dela Florida . . . Levantado . . . por Juan de Liguera . . . 1742*. Madrid, Depot de la Guerra. Photostat in the Library of Congress). Just when the transition from Jove to Jupiter took place cannot certainly be ascertained, but it was probably at the time of the ingress of the English land-seekers, after the cession of Florida to Great Britain in 1763. Owing to the Englishman's propensity to anglicize proper names where found, "Jove" might easily have become "Jupiter." The name Grenville may have been that of a large landowner in the neighborhood, who obtained his grant directly from the British crown, and upon which he bestowed his own name "Grenville," though there is no record of such a grant in the lists of the East Florida grantees. The name Hoe-Bay that Dickinson gave to the chief village of the Jobeses is merely an Englishman's pronunciation of the Spanish word "Jobe." Thus the names Jobe, Hoe-Bay, and Jobeses, given to river, village, and tribe are all related terms.

The narrative portrays the Jobeses as brutal, truculent, and sanguinary people, who received the Dickinson company with demonstrations of intense anger and hostility. In this respect they were like the Tequesta, with whom they may have been connected both racially and linguistically. The term Jeaga, if it were ever used, can be applied at most to but three or four tribes, of which the Jobeses were one, each with its village, for in addition to Hoe-Bay there are only two other Indian villages mentioned by Dickinson as lying between the River Jobe and St. Lucie Inlet. That the Rio Jobe (later Jupiter Inlet but entering the ocean at a more southerly point) was open in Dickinson's day to boats of small draft, not only canoes but even the ship's longboat, is evident from the fact that Dickinson and a few others, instead of rowing up the sound or inland river (now Hobe Sound), went outside along the shore in the ship's boat, which had been brought from the place of shipwreck across the bar into the inlet, and that too with the boat heavily loaded.

That the Jobeses, with all their ferocity, were an inferior and subordinate group of Indians is shown not only from the fact that the more aggressive cacique at Ais was able to wrest from the cacique at Hoe-Bay a part at least of the plunder from the shipwrecked vessel, but also from the further fact that the Hoe-Bay village followed a more primitive pattern of protective construction than did the town of Ais. The former was made up of small wigwams, framed with poles set in the ground, bent so as to form an arch, and covered with a thatch of small palmetto leaves. This was the simplest type of an Indian tepee, and as with all Indian dwellings of this kind was not designed for prolonged or permanent occupation.

As was true of all Indians south of Cape Canaveral, the Jobeses were not an agricultural people, a fact that clearly appears from the character of their wigwams and their manner of life. They were not tillers of the soil, neither sowing nor reaping, as Dickinson says, but were dependent on whatever nature provided for sustenance. They obtained their food from the fish which they speared freely in the daytime and with the aid of torches at night, from oysters, clams, crabs, and crawfish, from the starch pith of the coontie root (one reads of "Koontie and Hunting Grounds" in southern Florida and knows that coontie starch-making later became a profitable industry), from aquatic plants and berries—the last named chiefly clusters of sea-grapes, prickly pears, coco plums (white and pink), and pigeon plums—and from the hearts and berries of the palmetto, all of which were eaten both fresh and dried and in either form were thoroughly disliked by the Dickinson company. Unlike the Timucuas to the north, the Jobeses seem to have made little use of meat, for they rejected the beef and pork that the *Reformation* carried. Though the fruiting season lasted well into October, most of the berries were gone by that time and the Indians were dependent, until spring came again, on fish, oysters, and roots, and possibly on such animal flesh as they could bludgeon or kill with bows and arrows. The expression found on the various title-pages of the *Journal* "the Inhuman canibals of Florida" may well have expressed a fear rather than a reality. They were greedily fond of tobacco, as Dickinson tells us, thus confirming what Hawkins had said of the Timucuas a century before, but whether they found it growing wild or smoked a dried herb of a similar nature is equally uncertain, though the avidity with which they took tobacco from the white man makes it doubtful if they had any of their own. They drank a liquor called casseena. Dickinson has a description of the method of its manufacture, though he does not tell us the name of the leaves from which the liquor was brewed or distilled. The name may be Spanish, but whether applied to the shrub from which the leaves were

obtained or to the drink itself is not clear. Oddly enough, the
Indians seem to have had no desire to try the strong drink of
the English and ignored it when looting the cargo.

North of the Jobeses and the two or three related tribes
lying between Lake Worth and St. Lucie Inlet, were the Ais
or Ays, a warlike people, whose chief town was Ais, which
may have given its name to the Inlet of Ais ("Escudo de Aix,"
as Sanson's map of 1657 has it) or vice versa, though the inlet,
which is mentioned on a map as late as 1777, is not certainly
identical with St. Lucie Inlet. This town of Ais may be identified tentatively with the Jece of the narrative, where the
company remained for more than a month. The town was two
leagues north of Indian River Inlet and some little distance
away from the coast. The Province of Ais was well known to
the Spaniards and at one time had been under their control,
and the River of Ais is the same as that now known as the
Indian River. The exact location of the town is not yet certainly established, despite recent archeological attempts to
discover its site. It was more substantially built than was the
village of Hoe-Bay, though, even so, it did not prove very re-
sistant to the weather, for in the storm that occurred while
Dickinson was there some of the houses were much injured,
lying knee deep in water, while others were blown away by the
wind. But whatever differences may have existed between the
tepees of Hoe-Bay and the wooden houses of Ais there was but
little difference between the two groups of Indians themselves.
They were both at bottom cowardly, tricky, and belligerent
people, even though Dickinson does give evidence of a meas-
ure of kindliness and humane feeling among them, notably
among the caciques and their wives and occasionally among
the people themselves.

The fear the Indians had of the Spanish, though largely
traditional, may have been increased by occasional contacts,
however rare these may have been. A Jesuit mission had existed at Santa Lucea or St. Lucie (the name discloses the
Spanish connection) in the sixteenth century, though it had
long since been abandoned. The labors of the Franciscans,

confined in Dickinson's day to the north and west of St. Augustine, could easily have become matters of distant repute, for the Jesuits of the sixteenth century and the friars later made many efforts to convert the natives wherever found —on Biscayne Bay, at the town of Carlos, at Santa Lucea, and in the north. An early friar learned the language of the Timucuan Indians and made a dictionary of it about 1602. These efforts could hardly have been forgotten among a people dependent on mouth-to-mouth communication. Menéndez had gone on foot with a few companions from St. Augustine to Ais in 1565, suffering much from hunger and fatigue, and had remained there a few days before departing for Cuba. Remembrance of this exploit could well have remained deeply imbedded in the Indian mind. Military officials had penetrated among the Indians to the southward of St. Augustine, had interviewed their caciques, and at times had engaged in punitive expeditions, followed by conferences and peace. But whatever the results may have been there is no reason to believe that the Indians of Hoe-Bay knew much about either Englishmen or Spaniards, from personal association, for all the evidence goes to show that in the early seventeenth century they had had very few opportunities to meet the white man. It is worthy of note that Dickinson, although he says that one of the Indians whom he met north of Hoe-Bay spoke a little Spanish, records no contact with any Spaniards until more than five weeks had passed, and then only with a Spanish coast patrol that had come from the north summoned by one of the party, Solomon Cresson, who had been sent ahead to obtain assistance. It must be remembered that by 1696 Spanish control in Florida had shrunk to but a small part of the vast domain originally claimed by the crown and occupied by its missionaries and soldiers. In that year there was but one established sentry post south of Matanzas Inlet and there were no missionaries except in the neighborhood of St. Augustine.

The questions naturally arise as to why in the seventeenth century these Florida Indians entertained such strong sentiments of hostility toward the English and so wholesome a respect for the Spaniards; and further why it was that the Dickinson party, made up largely of English people, should have been received by the Spaniards themselves with such manifestations of friendship and good will. It is not difficult to find answers to each of these questions. As to the first, it will be recalled that in the first sixty years of the seventeenth century an intense bitterness of feeling existed between England and Spain, an abiding hostility that must have been known to the Indians and have made a deep impression upon their imagination; and that less than forty years had passed since the English had attacked Hispaniola (Santo Domingo) and had conquered Jamaica, incidents in Cromwell's famous Western Expedition of 1654. This naval and military exploit was designed to drive out the Spaniards from the colonies that Spain possessed in the Caribbean and to convert as many of them as possible into English Protestant dependencies.

The knowledge of an old-time animosity between the two countries may well have come to the Indians either from the Spanish in Florida, whose antipathy can be traced back to the English attack on St. Augustine in the sixteenth century, or by way of Cuba, where efforts to recover Jamaica continued for some years after the Conquest. Familiarity with such a situation, created by a remembrance of things past and strengthened by rumor passing from tribe to tribe, and filtering down from the Spanish in Florida could have become an established conviction with the Indians. Dickinson speaks of reports thus running from Indian town to Indian town.

This being the case, how are we to answer the second question and explain the kind reception the members of the Dickinson party experienced first at the hands of the Spanish coast patrol sent to assist them and afterward from the Spanish governor at St. Augustine? Though the latter, soon after their arrival, warned them to be careful in going about the city, as there still existed many who "did not affect our nation" (the English), he himself did everything in his power to make them comfortable and to relieve their wants. I believe that this change of mind was due to the terms of the important treaty signed at Madrid between England and Spain in 1670.

This treaty, which closed the aftermath of the Thirty Years' War, was distinctly favorable to England and disadvantageous to Spain. Spain was in no position to resist the English demands. This treaty brought to the two countries a temporary peace based on the acceptance by each of the colonial possessions actually held at the time by the other. It guaranteed kind entertainment in Spanish colonial ports for English vessels in distress and for English subjects in distress also, in which category the Dickinson party certainly found itself. The Spanish governor at St. Augustine would have received the terms of this treaty, as a matter of course, through the official channels as a part of his instructions, but of the change which had taken place in the relations between the two countries the Indians of central Florida could hardly have had an inkling. To them the English were still the enemies of Spain. Their memories would be tenacious of the old hostility, which antedated the treaty of 1670, the terms of which they could not have understood even if they had known of them. As far as the main body of the Indians was concerned there was no way in which information of this kind could have been imparted, and even the caciques themselves could not have had news of the treaty before the arrival of Sebastian Lopez and his soldiers at Jece, while Dickinson was there. The latter on that occasion speaks of the Spaniards as "extraordinarily kind to us," and of Lopez as "looking over a paper often, which we supposed was the governor's order and instructions to him." It is not difficult to believe that this "order and instructions" had some connection with the terms of the treaty of 1670.

The Indians had a word "Espania," which to their minds connoted the whole quintessence of Spanish mightiness and stood significantly opposed to the word "Nickaleer," which, contrariwise, stood for the English as the enemies of Spain. As far as we know, their acquaintance with the English themselves had been confined to such mariners as were cast upon their shores and had fallen victims to their rapacity. On the other hand, of the Spaniards they knew a good deal though remotely. They had heard of Havana and St. Augustine and were aware of the direction in which each lay. They readily distinguished between the two peoples in the matter of hair and complexion. Some of them apparently could recognize an occasional Spanish word, and a few could use enough words to be understood. Dickinson speaks of the cacique at Jece as an ancient man, his beard and hair gray, who could use the language "better than any we had met with yet." Santa Lucea had been a Jesuit mission and the Franciscans never stopped in their endeavor to learn the Indian language, and in the effort must have let drop at least a minimum of Spanish words. The northern Timucuas spoke Spanish and could identify Englishmen, Frenchmen, and Spaniards from their speech and contrasting appearances. The Jobeses had Spanish knives, which they might, it is true, have obtained from the spoils of English and Dutch vessels, and pistareens are reported to have been found along the beach near Jupiter Inlet. They knew something of a Spanish ceremony and their caciques had a sense of the value of money, the hard money of Spain, and coveted the contents of trunks, chests, and boxes, which contained for them varieties of clothes, hatchets, knives, and other implements, some of which could be utilized in Indian warfare. This covetousness is shown by their eagerness to filch what they wanted of the goods strewn along their shores. Just what they could do with the money and with the clothing which they so greedily seized from the wreckage or tore off the bodies of the unfortunate people who fell among them is not clear, for their own attire and the equipment of their villages show an extreme paucity of covering and adornment. Possibly the caciques had an eye to decoration, for we read elsewhere of one of them wearing a torque of gold, and early explorers speak of gold ornaments and of gold and silver which Indians willingly exchanged for tobacco and the like, but where the gold came from and how it was worked up we do not know certainly. It may have come from the wrecks of Spanish galleons or those of the buccaneers who frequented the coast, and as a malleable metal have been shaped by hammering. As a rule Indian ornamentation was confined to shells and other easily obtainable trinkets. Still the wives of the caciques may have had higher ambitions regarding the clothes they wore. In a letter to his wife Robert Barrow says that the Indians stripped the Dickinson party of their clothes to save them from being bloody when their owners were killed.

The Province of Ais extended north to the waters lying behind Cape Canaveral, where it abutted on the land of the Surruque (Sorroches according to the hydrographer, Le Moyne), the southernmost of the tribes of the Timucuas. The latter Indian people occupied the land from Cape Canaveral north to the present Florida-Georgia line and westward toward the Gulf of Mexico, where they met the Apalache. Unlike the lands of the Jobeses and the Ais, the territory occupied by the Timucuas was not limited to the eastern coast, but extended across the peninsula, with its center of authority at Santa Fé, where were a Franciscan mission and a presidio. Their most populous settlements were along the St. Johns River, from its mouth inland. The Dickinson narrative tells us of the Timucuan town of St. Wans, situated on an island at the mouth of the river, where were a Franciscan friar and a "worshipping house," and where the company remained for two days, "well fed" and living in an Indian "war-house."

In the sixteenth century the Timucuas had been a powerful people, made up of at least seven independent tribes, with seven separate but related dialects, the customs and manners of which are portrayed by the French Huguenot Jacques le Moyne de Morgues, who came over with Laudonniere and was the first artist to visit America. His work consists of a series of drawings depicting the outward appearance of the Timucuas, their towns, their ceremonials, and their methods of warfare. These drawings, of which but one original is known to exist (discovered in a French chateau in 1901), were engraved and somewhat embellished by Theodore De Bry and published at Frankfort in 1591, under the title the *Timucuan Indians of 1564*. Le Moyne was a forerunner of John White who, because of Raleigh's interest in both men, was influenced by Le Moyne's example. Twenty-three of White's drawings of the Virginia Indians, of which sixty-three originals are still extant, were also engraved by De Bry and published at Frankfort in 1590. Le Moyne's drawings, accompanied by a map and descriptive texts—the latter oddly enough in Italian for the benefit of the Italian members of the French court of Charles IX—bring to life a vanished Indian people.

The best account of the sixteenth century Timucuas is to be found in the narrative of a voyage by John Hawkins, who visited the St. Johns River while Laudonniere was there and had dealings with him on the spot. Hawkins describes the land as "wooded," with growths of cedar, cypress, and other varieties of trees, and mentions the cultivation of maize, the preparation of meal, the raising of grapes, the care of "fowls" and other poultry, the hunting of deer and "divers other beasts," the use of herbs in great variety, one of which was dried and smoked by the Indians in an earthenware cup with a long cane, a practice similar to that described by Dickinson. He speaks also of meadows and pastures. The Timucuan houses, he states, were well built, as strong as English houses, with stanchions and rafters of whole trees covered with palmetto leaves. Both he and Laudonniere had found the Bahama Channel "dangerous" because of "sundry banks." He comments on the "masts which were the wracks of Spaniards coming from Mexico," and to these "wracks" he ascribes the presence of gold and silver among the Indians, with which the latter used to buy what they wanted from the Frenchmen. He calls especial attention to the size of their canoes.

During the wars in which the Timucuas were engaged with the French and Spanish from 1518 to 1687, they were gradually reduced to the status of mission Indians, and later, remaining loyal to Spain, were defeated by the English and their Yemassee allies from South Carolina in the years from 1702 to 1706. Santa Fé was destroyed in 1702, and continued attacks completed the ruin and dispersion of the tribes. Retreating to the headwaters of the St. Johns River, they gradually lost their identity as a separate Indian people and since that time have entirely disappeared from history.